CW01501385

Table of Contents

1. WHY GARDEN IN CONTAINERS?

The idea for this book came during my first trip to Europe, eight years ago, when I was thrilled by the casual abundance of pot plants in the patios and courtyards of southern France, Italy, and Greece. In the cities and towns of northern France, England, Scotland, Belgium, Holland, and particularly Switzerland, I marveled at the window boxes of luxuriant red and pink geraniums.

Since then I have made two extended trips to Europe to visit other countries. In Portugal and Spain, I saw secluded patios, with rippling fountains and pools adorned with potted roses and carnations. Throughout Ireland, Austria, Germany, and the Scandinavian countries, I admired the countless window boxes filled with geraniums and tuberous begonias. All this left me with the thought that we, too, should use container plants with greater freedom.

One Plant, a Garden

It occurred to me that a single attractive container plant at a doorway or on a porch or balcony is enough to

Outdoor Gardening
In Pots and Boxes

George Taloumis

make a pot garden. The idea was strengthened one hot August afternoon when I saw a tub of Black Prince fuchsia gracing a simple colonial doorway. Similarly, the container garden might even comprise two specimen plants, as urns with clipped yews or clumps of geraniums.

Growing plants in containers is a distinctive form of gardening. It is particularly appealing because the plants can be moved about for a change of picture and mood. But it also has an architectural quality lacking in plants that are grown in the open ground. What garden sight is more delightful than a flight of stairs bedecked with pots of fiery red geraniums? Or what compares to a pool re-flecting great blue hydrangeas in tubs or urns or to window boxes overflowing with petunias high above the city streets.

In recent years, growing plants in movable or immovable containers-pots and tubs, window and plant boxes, planters, and hanging" baskets-has developed into a new gardening concept. In part, this is due to contemporary architecture, which presents numerous opportunities for the display of container plants around house and garden. Patios and terraces, paved walks, paths and driveways, planters, raised beds, and retaining walls are characteristic at today's new homes. Sun decks, barbecue areas, garden shelters, swimming pools, tennis and badminton

ILLUSTRATION I

Hanging baskets of ivy-leaved geraniums and concrete tubs of upright Japanese yews at the entrance of a colonial house.

ILLUSTRATION II
English ivy, pyramidally trained on wire forms, at the doorway of
Mrs. Craven Nichols. Pot plants like these will last several years.

courts, carports and private docks for boats are other indications
that Americans are spending more time outdoors. Although
container gardening is essentially old and timeless, it has evolved
to suit the needs of the day.

But why grow plants in containers when you can garden in the
ground? Aside from the advantage of mobility, it is easy to

discard and replace unsightly specimens and to avoid overcrowding, a problem in borders. At party time, new kinds can be introduced for color, foliage, or pattern effects. In addition, rare and unusual varieties and those with special soil, temperature, and light needs can be more easily cared for, while plants with small and delicate or fragrant flowers can be brought to close range. New kinds can also be tried out before they are placed in the garden.

Immediate Effects

Immediate effects can also be achieved with pot plants. When you plan a terrace party, you can purchase flowering or foliage specimens from florists or nurserymen to use where needed. Sometimes, cut blooms of large flowers -gladiolus, peonies, delphiniums, calla and other lilies, snapdragons and birds-of-paradise-can be inserted in bottles of water and then arranged in containers to look as if they were growing. To create this impression, cover the

ILLUSTRATION III
A tubbed standard geranium by the doorway of a charming house.
There is a similar specimen on the other side.

ILLUSTRATION IV

Glossy-leaved spathiphyllum in a tub at the side entrance of the home of Daniel J. Foley. This tropical plant requires a warm place in the winter.

tops of the bottles with sphagnum or peat moss. Or from the garden, you can lift and pot up annuals-petunias, marigolds, or ageratum-or perennials such as phlox, hardy asters, and chrysanthemums. Do this a little ahead to give plants time to adjust. Keep them in shade for the first few days and water frequently to avoid their drying out. Then arrange them for terrace decoration.

Saving Time

With containers, gardening chores-watering, feeding, weeding, staking, spraying, and removing faded blooms-are easily managed. To save time and energy, the wise enthusiast will keep his container plants concentrated in one, two, or three areas.

Water Scarcity

Where water is limited during the growing season, container gardening can be the solution. Hot, dry summers are responsible for the widespread practice in the Mediterranean countries, in Southern California, Arizona, and New Mexico, as well as in Mexico and other areas of similar climate. Gardeners who live where there is drought can also adopt the method, since sufficient water is usually available for pot plants.

After planting annuals in the spring, you can pot up

ILLUSTRATION V

Informal homemade wooden boxes with geraniums on the steps of a summer place.

the leftovers as a reserve supply for failures. Where Dutch bulbs are raised in containers outdoors (they need some protection where temperatures go below freezing), they can easily be removed after flowering to avoid the unsight-liness of ripening foliage. In the North, tender tropicals can be potted and treated as summer subjects and then brought in for the winter. The same plants can remain outdoors all year-round where the climate is sufficiently warm.

Plant-lovers, who live in rented houses or apartments and have no space to garden, or do not want to invest in permanent plants even if they have a place, can rely on potted plants. Then, if they decide to move during the growing season, the containers can be taken along to give a new house a lived-in appearance. Families living in trailers can also adopt the practice to advantage. Furthermore, animal pests are apt to be less troublesome to plants in containers, especially bulbs, some of which are sought by squirrels, moles, and gophers.

Those who wish can develop an entire container garden at waist level on specially built shelves or benches, on low walls or in raised beds and planters, with potting equipment and supplies stored in a nearby shed or cabinet. This arrangement eliminates stooping and bending and is fine

ILLUSTRATION VI

Clay pots covered with decorative baskets. The plant on the left is a
Martha Washington geranium; the other, a chrysanthemum.

ILLUSTRATION VII

Specimen shrimp plants at the front doorway of Mrs. Owen Moon. These
profuse flowering plants require regular pinching to keep them bushy.

ILLUSTRATION VIII

Golden Leaf euonymus and heart-leaved philodendron in a wall basket on a garden gate. Several types of containers are available for gates, fences and walls for the elderly and the afflicted who could not otherwise enjoy the pleasures of gardening.

For Meeting Places and Church Gardens

The pot gardener will find that he can perform a real civic service by lending his plants for club meetings, church gatherings, and other community affairs. An acquaintance, whose town was sponsoring an important concert, decorated the stage with handsome potted geraniums from her terrace. She placed them against a background of beech branches. The effect was so striking, she heard "about it for weeks afterwards."

Today many churches are establishing gardens on their grounds, often with the aid of community garden clubs. Large boxes planted with evergreens at the main entrance and tubs of geraniums and chrysanthemums at side doorways will contribute considerable charm to any place of worship. And in the garden itself, particularly if it is mainly green, pots of flowering plants-white lilies at Easter and golden chrysanthemums for fall-will be most attractive.

2. POT GARDENING - PAST AND PRESENT

Gardening in pots and other containers is apparently as old as civilization, for the practice can be traced to the very early use of medicinal and edible plants. In time, pot gardening developed to a high degree, and there are numerous records which reveal its importance in China, India, Egypt, Assyria, Greece, and Rome. Since ancient days, it has been particularly enjoyed in countries with hot, dry summers and low annual rainfall.

In tracing the history of pot gardening, we can go to paintings from the Middle Period in Egypt to see formal gardens with "beds marked out in squares like a chessboard." * In one illustration of a garden at El-Bersheh, there is a long "row of pot plants, an early example of ornament that, became common later on."

* This quotation and others in this chapter are from "A History of Gardening Art," Vols. I & II, by Marie Luise Gothein.

In Greece and Rome

In Greece, the so-called Adonis garden marked the beginning of pot gardening there. In midsummer, when Athenian women celebrated the Festival of Adonis, they placed around the statue of Adonis earthen pots filled with soil in which they sowed fennel and lettuce as well as wheat and barley. As time went on, the simple pagan custom became a children's game and boys who, "sowed quick-growing seeds in great pots," were delighted "when the green began to show." In the writings of Theophrastus, too, there are references to pot gardening.

In Imperial Rome, the court of Domitian at the Palatine was "adorned with flowers just as the Assyrians plant them on the roofs in honour of Adonis" and Domi-tian's palace was decorated with tubs placed all around the roof of the pillared court, a practice adopted later in Pompeii. Town houses had flower gardens in front of the windows, "very probably on wide balconies, which were attached to each story 'so that every day the eyes might feast on this copy of a garden, as though it were the work of nature.' " Boxes for growing plants were also attached to windows of Roman houses. Pliny, the Elder, in the first century, described the "mimic gardens" in the windows of Rome, and how they brought the country to the town.

Boxes for growing plants were also placed on roofs. Seneca wrote that on the high towers of Pompeii, "they planted fruit-trees and shrubberies, with roots where their tops ought to be." It was in Pompeii, too, that "a small nursery was discovered with a whole array of painted pots, presumably for raising seed or cuttings." Byzantine emperors likewise favored rooftop gardening, and a poem on Justinian I describes a little house that had "a balcony-garden with a lovely view of the sea."

Through the Middle Ages and the Renaissance

Though medicinal and edible plants were favored in the gardens of the Middle Ages, they were also ornamented with pot plants. Exotics were frequently planted in containers to make them "objects of beauty," and gardeners practiced "the curious custom of placing pots and growing flowers on beds already planted with flowers," particularly carnations, which were favorites. During the Renaissance in Italy and later in France, England, and elsewhere, pot plants became common garden features. On a roof garden in Verona, plants in square tubs, in-cluding cypresses, were arranged around geometric beds. Many of the famed Italian villa gardens introduced decorative pots and urns with oranges, lemons, oleanders, and sweet bay, a practice that continues today. At Villa D'Este

at Tivoli pots adorned the broad walls, and there were urns rilled with plants of many kinds. Hundreds of container plants were also used at Villa Aldobrandini at Frascati, where the stairs were "gay with oranges in pots." At Isola Bella, the fascinating terraced gardens, with their numerous pot plants, never fail to delight visitors today.

In Spain

In a sense, pot gardening came into its own in the gardens of Spain. Under the Moors, life in Spain was Oriental. The gardens, with their fountains and ornamental flower pots, were open living-rooms. Similar outdoor living areas developed in Portugal, which was also occupied by the Moors.

From the time of the Renaissance, when the Italian style of gardening was adopted in northern Europe, potted plants and decorative urns were important. When Versailles set the fashion for the rest of Europe, its fabulous gardens, with their tubbed orange trees and elegant urns, were also copied.

Through Germany and Holland

In Germany, there was a strong trend toward pot gardening. According to a sketch of the seventeenth-century garden of Christopher Peller in *Nurenberg,* urns and potswere lavishly scattered about. Around the beds, "there are lower stone borders with ornamental pots set on them: these contain plants of many kinds, with orange-trees and other costly foreign plants that have to pass the winter in a hothouse."

A garden of the same date belonging to Johannes Schwindt, a burgomaster of Frankfort, comprised an enclosure "made of green lattice-work with pillars, windows, and gates," with pots of flowering plants at the windows and on benches.

A visitor to Holland in 1812, described a typical planting at the village of Broek: "The gardens in front of their houses are just as wonderful to look at. You can find everything there except nature . . . trees ... no longer look like trees so clipped are their tops." Areas between flower beds "are filled with coloured glass beads, shells, stones, and pots in all manners of colours."

In the Orient

Pot plants were always much used in the East, especially in Chinese gardens, where the emphasis is on pines, foliage plants, and decorated vessels. Commonly grown in vases and containers were dwarf trees, "a main occupation of Chinese gardeners." In China, and elsewhere in eastern countries, the houses adjoin courts, which are given character with "flowering trees and shrubs, or pot plants, which are liked still more."

In early as well as advanced cultures, growing plants in containers has been a universal practice, a symbol of man's innate love and need for growing things. Wherever soil was lacking or the climate was unfavorable, containers made it possible to enjoy the beauty and inspiration of plants. Today, the practice continues to grow, ever changing to fit the needs of the time.

IN EUROPE TODAY

American visitors to the Old World are invariably impressed by the exuberant displays of container plants around homes, in gardens and parks, and in front of public buildings and places of business.

In Lisbon, with its narrow, winding streets, where there is hardly a trickle of sunlight, windowsills and tiny balconies are filled with potted plants. Often, they must compete with clothes hung out to dry. I recall one small balcony that contained numerous pot plants, several pieces of laundry, six song birds in cages, and three shouting green parrots attached to their perches by chains.

Throughout Portugal, containers range from tin cans, clay and decorated glazed pots at entranceways and in small patios, to large cast-stone urns and pots in elegant,formal gardens, like that of the Queluz Palace outside Lisbon. In the moister north, pot plants are seen less frequently than in the hot and dry south, which has a more typically Mediterranean climate.

The countless pot plants around fountains and pools in the Moorish gardens at the Alhambra and Generaliffe Palaces in Granada are unforgettable. At Generaliffe, they are arranged so precisely and symmetrically along the long, narrow canals that they are almost as diverting as the numberless fountains that leap and splash in these gardens where water in its myriad forms plays so important a part. Along the narrow streets of Seville and other Spanish cities, geraniums and climbing roses grow through the intricate lacework of little balconies. Patios, surrounded by high walls, are crammed with potted geraniums, stocks, lemons, oranges, boxwood, sweet bay, jasmines, and Swedish myrtle. Even more, steps are lined with pots of all sizes and descriptions and the tops of walls, also favorite places, resemble miniature gardens.

Italian and Greek Use

The Italian garden would be incomplete without potlants. In the terraced gardens of La Mortola in Ventiiglia and Borremeo Castle on Iseo Bello in Lake Magiore, in the extensive Boboli Gardens in Florence, andin other villa gardens throughout Italy, handsomely designed hand-wrought clay pots are important aspects of the designs. Lemons and oranges, oleanders, gardenias, and geraniums are grown in them.

Around the bay of Naples and along the Italian Riviera, fiery red and pink ivy-leaved geraniums cascade from balconies.

In sooty, industrial Milan, Virginia creeper and wisteria vines dominate large boxes on the balconies of new apartment houses. In Sicily, under conditions of poverty and limited space, pot plants still are in evidence, often on shelves suspended on walls or over the doors of one-room houses.

Greece, with its hot, dry summers, is equally a country of gardens and open courtyards of pot plants. In tin cans, whitewashed or painted yellow, pink, or blue to match the house, the Greeks grow their beloved carnations, stocks, gardenias, geraniums, jasmines, and particularly basil, the pungent Indian herb used for flavoring. When immigrants came to America earlier in the century, they brought with them the practice of growing basil and fragrant flowering plants in tins and other makeshift containers.

In Greece, as in Spain, patios and terraces express a way of life. For many, they afford the only place to grow such favorites as aspidistra, elephant's ear, clivia, monstera, ruscus, China asters, cosmos, and marguerites. Modern suburban gardens, with facilities for watering, have fewer pots; but balconies are packed with them. In Ellini-con, a small village in the Peloponnesus, the fragrant white-flowering August lily *(Hosta plantaginea),* known also as Corfu lily, is everybody's cherished possession, even supplanting basil.

Through France and Scandinavia

The south of Prance, with its warm climate, follows the pattern of Portugal, Spain, Italy, and Greece. In the north, including Paris, pots, often of house plants, rest on windowsills and adorn courtyards. In formal chateaux and palace gardens, tubbed sweet bay, oleander, and orange and lemon trees are common, along with ornamental urns, introduced for architectural effect. Window boxes, with geraniums and tuberous begonias, predominate in Switzerland, Germany, and Austria.

In Scandinavia, there are large plant containers in public squares and on broad sidewalks, in fact, wherever they do not interfere with pedestrian traffic. In front of City Hall in the heart of Copenhagen, great concrete containers with geraniums and other summer flowers are grouped among the benches where people sit in the sun. These modern containers can be seen in the parks and squaresof Stockholm and other Scandinavian cities. Shaped like inverted bells, they are planted with colorful tulips and azaleas in the spring, geraniums and white and yellow marguerites in the summer, and chrysanthemums in the fall.

In the Low Countries and Britain

In the cities and gardens of Belgium and Holland, there is not the rich display of other countries, though tubbed sweet bay, oleander, hydrangea, pomegranate, and such tropicals as palms and rubber plants, command attention in old gardens and public parks. In Amsterdam, shallow square and rectangular containers, resembling enormous pans, enliven sidewalks, with their masses of tulips and other spring bulbs. Raised in flats, the bulbs are placed close together for dramatic effect. In Amsterdam in May there are groups of concrete containers with yellow-flowering cytisus or broom.

London, Dublin, and Edinburgh have window boxes and urns that decorate banks, department stores, public buildings, and offices. Azaleas and other spring flowers are followed by hydrangeas and geraniums in the summer and chrysanthemums in the autumn. Plant boxes are often placed on top of department store marquees. These are also a familiar sight in Paris.

Attractive container plants, like the tubs of agapanthus around the pools at Hampton Court, highlight walks, steps, terraces, verandas, walls, balustrades, and summer houses of English gardens. In Ireland, many pot plants grace the windows of thatch-roofed cottages. The favorites are geraniums and oxalis, a three-leafed plant that suggests the beloved shamrock.

But it is in southern Europe that pot plants are used with extravagant profusion and gay abandon. Along walls or balustrades, next to splashing pools and fountains, around courtyard entrances, or balconies and rooftops, on steps and stairs, along walks and paths, on patios and terraces, beside doorways and on top of low or high walls, they are scattered with carefree casualness befitting the climate, the tradition, and especially the way of life.

In all these countries, with their centuries of experience, we can find ideas to adapt to our own climate, styles of architecture, and manner of gardening. The multitude of containers and plants offer many possibilities for adding architectural accent and introducing a distinctive kind of garden beauty.

3. PLACES FOR POTS AND PLANTERS

Nearly every house and garden presents numerous attractive settings for container plants. Suburban gardens, estates, small city backyards, and summer cottages-all can be enhanced by this type of gardening. A few of the seemingly endless possibilities include entranceways, steps, courtyards, walls, rooftops, balconies, patios, breezeways, lawns, driveways, walks, sundecks, windowsills, porches, summer houses, even tree stumps.

Let us start with the entrance, a focal point for every house. A simple arrangement consists of similar container plants at each side of the doorway. H the house is informal, painted tubs will make a cheerful note, while urns or ornamental pots are more appropriate if the architecture is formal. The arrangement, however, need not be symmetrical, since a single container at either side, particularly if the doorway is off-center, is pleasing. A large specimen can be balanced by a grouping of small pots, and various other interesting combinations can be worked out. Sometimes, the front entranceway can qualify as asummering-out place for house plants, especially if they are not exposed to strong sun and wind.

Side and rear entrances can also serve as backgrounds for pot plants in casual groupings. For sunny steps, consider tubs of petunias, or dwarf dahlias, or boxes of herbs to be used in cooking. Tuberous begonias, fuchsias, patient Lucy, and fragrant nicotiana solve the problem of what to grow in shade.

Porches and Patios

Porches or verandas, traditional or contemporary in style, offer numerous settings for pots, window boxes, and hanging baskets. Indeed, the entire container garden can be concentrated there so that plants can be easily cared for. If the porch is open on three sides, it will afford exposures to suit a variety of specimens.

The patio or terrace, beside or beyond the house, where family and friends gather to eat or rest, is an ideal location. If it is formal, select clipped evergreens and arrange pots in symmetrical rows, perhaps lined up against the house or along the edge of the terrace. If the site is informal, make casual groupings of one or two tall plants with smaller ones in front. Either way, allow for a few large plants in tubs or boxes for accent and height.

ILLUSTRATION IX

Potted tree heliotropes and geraniums on the picturesque well
head in the small city garden of Mr. and Mrs. Charles Townsend
of Beacon Hill, Boston.

ILLUSTRATION X

Tree fuchsia and potted pink geraniums on the balcony and terrace of the courtyard of Mr. and Mrs. Charles Townsend on Boston's historic Beacon Hill.

Walks and Driveways

Container plants may line walks and paths that lead to the house, garage, or garden. They can rest on paved areas along fences and walls and on driveways where they are not in the way.

If the driveway adjoins the foundation of the house, plant containers may be placed there. In their small city lot, Mr. and Mrs. Moses Alpers of Salem, Massachusetts, closed off their driveway with two three-foot wooden, custom-made planters and joined them with a low picket gate that serves as an entrance. The driveway area beyond, transformed into a summer terrace, is decorated with pots of geraniums, heliotropes, passion plants, and tomato vines. Lounge chairs are stored in winter in the unused garage, which also provides storage space for the planters which have wheels.

Tops of Walls

Tops of garden or terrace walls are ideal places, too. Put small pots and boxes on tall, narrow walls and large containers on low, broad surfaces. Hanging plants of ivy geraniums in the sun and fuchsias in the shade will cascade from walls, as they do in the patios of Spain, Portugal, and Italy. On Rhodes, I recall a fifteen-foot walltopped with a row of thirty gleaming green tin cans full of roses and other flowers.

Rooftops and Sundecks

Think of what you can do with rooftops and sundecks where considerable space is usually available. Here sun-loving plants, like geraniums, most annuals, cacti, and succulents can be grown, but, again, include large specimens for height to give a garden feeling. A few large boxes and planters for trees and shrubs are sufficient but be sure to include some evergreens for year-round green.

In Flower Borders

Some gardeners like to insert container plants in flower borders to introduce unusual specimens, such as tropicals in the North. Large tubs can be set at the corners and small pots may be scattered among the permanent flowering plants. One gardener keeps a supply of potted pink Fiat Enchantress geraniums on hand to fill bare spots in her wide borders, moving them about as needed. Most of the geraniums are in four-inch clay pots, but there are larger specimens for the center of each grouping. To make them secure, pots are sunk a few inches into the ground.

ILLUSTRATION XI

Double white petunias and pink geraniums in a white window box attached to the yellow house of Mr. and Mrs. C. A. B. Halvorson. The same flowers are repeated in the clay pots below.

Around Lamp Posts

You can always dress up the lamp post in your yard with container plants at the base or you can suspend a hanging basket of lantana, perhaps from the top. Ivy geraniums in an old-fashioned black kettle are nice for the base. Bare posts that support sectional roofs over patios or paved surfaces of contemporary houses look more attractive if pot plants are clustered around the bases or permanent boxes for plants are built there.

For Lawns and Steps

Novelty containers-donkey carts, wheelbarrows, and spinning wheels-can be fun in some places, but, of course, such planters must not be overdone. Usually they are set on lawns, on a terrace or beside a gate or doorway. Steps leading to a driveway or street or to different levels in a garden can be emphasized with pot plants. A few can be arranged at the top or at the base of the stairs. And, there are other possibilities. Tree trunks cut to the ground or left a few feet high make good pedestals for large containers. In fact, this can be a solution to the problem of what to do with a trunk too expensive to remove. If you have a tree with heavy shade, why not construct a sitting area around it and decorate the space with pots of coleus, wax and other begonias, caladiums, ferns and other shade-tolerant plants.

4. CONTAINERS UNLIMITED - POTS, KETTLES, PLANTERS, BASKETS

An unlimited variety of containers is available for your garden. These range in size from small house-plant pots to large boxes and planters. Equally variable are the materials from which they are made. These include wood, glass, clay, aluminum, bamboo, straw, plastic, fiberglass, terra cotta, tin, cast iron, zinc, copper, and brass, each with certain advantages and disadvantages. What you select will depend on availability, cost, background, and appeal.

In addition to traditional circular pots and tubs, there are modern and ultra-modern forms-square, rectangular, triangular, hexagonal, and octagonal. Also eligible are old iron kitchen pots, kettles, pails, jugs, casks, vases, crocks, jelly tubs, barrels and nail kegs, Japanese fish tubs, old sinks, bathtubs, bamboo soy tubs, and novelties such as driftwood, wheelbarrows, donkey carts, spinning wheels and boxes attached to roadside mail boxes. There are also bird cages, decorative well heads, animal figures, and strawberry jars. Woven baskets may be used to conceal unattractive containers. Even tar paper pots, handled by nurserymen and florists, are worthwhile if painted or covered to improve their appearance.

Search Attics and Cellars

Start with what you have. If you scout cellars or basements, attics, garages, and sheds, you will doubtless encounter something interesting. Old-fashioned pots and kettles, often sold in antique shops at country auctions or seen at old New England inns, have much appeal.

Consider old cookie and bean jars, pickle and other types of crocks, wash tubs, coal pails, jardinieres, and ceramic bowls. For drainage, spread a thick layer of large pebbles or broken pieces of pots or bricks at the bottom and then water plants with care. In large containers of this kind, drainage material should be several inches thick. Where rainfall is heavy, it is advisable to keep containers without drainage outlets on porches or under awnings or the broad eaves of houses. With pails and old galvanized wash tubs, holes can be easily punctured at the bottom.

Plants in containers without drainage openings remain moist longer. Some of these-crocks, jardinieres and cookie jars-are heavy enough to be secure against wind. Earthy in character, they harmonize with geraniums, ice plants, cacti, and succulents. Yet others-iron pots, kettles, and pans-do not break and can be painted.

Ideal Container

What constitutes the ideal container? A container must be attractive, even if it is not an object of art. It should be strong and durable and able to resist all kinds of weather. This is especially true of the large sizes, which usually remain outdoors all year around. In the North, alternate freezing and thawing is a problem in winter; in tropical climates, excessive heat, humidity, and moisture are to be considered. And in semiarid areas, there is the effect of scorching sun to keep in mind.

The ideal container must be large enough to hold a substantial amount of soil. It should have good drainage facilities through holes or other openings at the bottom or sides, though this is not absolutely necessary. It must not rust, at least in a single season, and it should have a wide enough base to rest firmly wherever placed. Besides, it ought to be heavy enough to withstand average winds. In severe storms, movable containers can be shifted to temporary safety.

Durability

Resistance to rot is another requirement. Wooden containers-except those made of rot-resistant redwood, Western cedar, and Southern red cypress-will need to be treated with a wood preservative. Except for permanent containers, movability is another feature of the portable garden. Large boxes and planters can be fitted with wheels, and garden centers have redwood tubs that rest on platforms with wheels. A hole in the platform corresponds to the hole in the tub. Large containers without wheels can be pushed on iron or wooden rollers by two or more persons.

Clay Pots

Common unglazed clay pots make good starters because they are readily available and go well with all kinds of plants. Made of natural clay, they acquire a neutral color with age, even though they are harsh orange-red when new. One gardener gives them a mellow look by dunking them in a tub of manure water. On the other hand, clay pots become dirty with accumulations of white fertilizer salts and mosses, but they are easily cleaned by scrubbing with a stiff brush and sudsy water.

Unglazed clay pots are inexpensive, so you can keepa supply on hand. Since they are easily broken, you must guard them against wind, pulled garden hoses, and dogs. Place them at a safe distance from pedestrian traffic on steps, walks, or other passageways. Stained small pots can be broken into pieces for drainage material. Clay pots vary in size and ornamentation. The large decorated types, planted with lemons, oranges, and oleanders in Italian villa gardens, are also obtainable in this country.

Porous unglazed clay pots insure good aeration and proper drying out of the soil. Yet they often dry out too quickly, more quickly than glazed or wooden containers. In hot weather, plants may require watering in the morning and again in the evening, especially if they are pot bound. Actually, clay pots can lose twice as much moisture through their sides as through the soil surface. A properly prepared soil, with humus or other organic material plus a mulch of peat moss or pebbles, will cut the loss of moisture. For cacti and succulents these pots are ideal.

Dry clay pots, painted before they are planted, will be less porous and in some cases more attractive. If different colors are used each year, the container garden will not be dull. Desirable among clay pots are the small Italian types, characterized by simple circular rims. Large Italian pots, decorated richly with garlands, are indeed handsome and the gardener with the proper setting for them is fortunate.

Glazed Containers

For your garden, you might prefer glazed ceramic pots. Like jardinieres, they usually lack drainage holes and are most useful when unglazed pots are slipped inside them. These then do not dry out so quickly. Always be certain the potted plant stands above drainage water by placing pebbles, stones, or pieces of wood at the bottom of the jardiniere.

Glazed pots with drainage holes have several advantages. Plants require less frequent watering because the soil remains moist longer and surfaces of containers remain free of salt accumulations. On the other hand, watering requires care, though with practice you can learn just how much water to apply and when. Glazed pots come in many colors, but delicate pastel shades-pink, peach, aqua, or yellow-are usually preferred. For instance try pink geraniums in pink, soft green, or pale blue containers.

Glazed containers may be gaily decorated with intricate patterns or designs. These are seen in the patios of Portugal, Spain, and Italy as well as in Japanese gardens. In certain settings they may be appropriate with flowering plants, but they are best suited to foliage types, since the decorations detract from the flowers. In a Portuguese jardiniere or a Japanese porcelain urn, you will like sprenger asparagus, Japanese privet, rubber plant, French ivy, upright philodendron, cast iron plant, rosemary, or a foliage begonia.

Tubs Are Popular

Tubs-the traditional circular or the modern square, triangular, or hexagonal type-are outstanding plant containers. Easily available as well as durable, they are heavy when filled with soil, so they are not easily knocked over. Wooden containers can be painted; in fact, they can be given a different color each year, a pleasant chore for the winter. Wooden tubs can also be stained or allowed to weather naturally, and these are recommended for foliage plants, scented geraniums, and such herbs as rosemary, basil, chives, and sage.

The familiar circular wooden tub is widely accepted. Newer angular boxes-square, rectangular, triangular, octagonal, or hexagonal-have been designed for contemporary houses. These may be purchased or custom-made, generally in redwood, cedar, or Southern red cypress. Allowed to weather, they become a neutral gray, a color that goes with all flowering and foliage plants. But if desired, these woods may be painted or stained.

Wooden tubs, long lasting when treated to resist decay, hold moisture well. They also keep out the heat of the sun, preventing overheating of soil. Then, too, wood, substantial and solid in appearance, is well suited to formal or informal gardens.

Wooden Barrels

Barrels, oldtime standbys, are always excellent. Unless you prefer the full barrel shape, simply cut off the top at the desired height. Then bore holes at the bottom and paint the inside with a wood preservative. If the hoops are galvanized, they will not rust; if not, they will. To prevent this, apply oil or paint outside of the barrel. Hoops, which tend to slip, can be secured with nails.

Wooden boxes are becoming more and more the thing for the modern terrace. Varying in size and shape, large units are planted with trees, shrubs, and vines. The smaller sizes are allotted to perennials, herbs, and bulbs. Long planter boxes, intended for terraces, walks or driveways, can be filled with evergreens and blooming plants. When flowers-petunias, wax begonias or dwarf geraniums-are massed in large, low boxes they give the containers the look of garden beds.

Black locust, osage orange, and chestnut are other woods that do not rot if left untreated. To prevent boxes from resting directly on solid surfaces and thus stopping good drainage, raise them on short lifts or legs. Better still are wheels, for then the boxes can be pushed about.

Make Your Own

When possible, construct boxes to fit your needs. For example, a long, narrow box can be built for the driveway area adjacent to the house. If raised a few feet, it will be easier to care for. For that matter, you can make the box in units that are small enough to be easily moved and stored in winter.

Long boxes can be constructed for the front of the house to give interest and avoid the monotony of the traditional foundation planting. Or modular boxes of the same size can be arranged in a row for a pleasant effect. You can also make boxes of special shapes and sizes to fit around your swimming pool, on your terrace, or in front of a fence or tool house. Planters are also well adapted to small city or rooftop gardens.

In some instances, boxes can be tiered in front of a house or along a garage or fence for the sake of variety. A large box, with a shade or flowering tree, can give accent to a terrace or a doorway. Best of all, plant boxes canserve to guide traffic in the garden and through the outdoor living area. Some gardeners also like to maintain two or more sets of boxes to replace those with plants past their prime. This plan gives the gardener the fullest value from his portable garden.

Plastic Pots

Plastic pots, often preferred by growers of house plants, are attractive, lightweight, and water retentive. Available in neutral grays, greens, and black, they do not gather fertilizer salts on their surfaces. In clay pots, roots concentrate along the sides where water and nitrogen collect; in plastic, roots are distributed throughout the soil area. Yet plastic pots are not always practical because they are easily knocked over. The larger sizes, of course, are more secure.

One way to make plastic pots heavier is to slip them into clay pots, jardinieres, or wooden tubs or boxes. Another method is to arrange them in sheltered locations, grouped for support. On the other hand, they make desirable hanging baskets because they are light and attractive.

Urns for Grace

Urns, whether decorated or plain, are charming containers. Often they are used as a pair at each side of adoorway or driveway entrance, but just a single specimen will enhance a terrace or a garden nook. Urns are often made of cast iron, but clay and concrete are also used. In old palace gardens of Europe-at Versailles and Quelez, outside Lisbon-urns were important accents, and they may be seen today gracing these lovely, elegant formal gardens.

Concrete Containers

Sturdy concrete containers have a solid appearance. They do not topple in strong winds or crack where winters are cold. Usually they are left outdoors all year to ornament house, shop, or hotel. Concrete containers may be plain or highly ornamented, and what you select will depend on the setting. Though generally purchased, they can be custom made in small sizes for geraniums, petunias, and other flowers or in large sizes for evergreens-as arborvitae, yews, Japanese privet, aucuba, camellia, pittos-porum, or holly. These are often placed in front of large apartments, hotels, restaurants, department stores, and public buildings.Plants grow well in concrete containers because thesoil remains moist and the roots cool. As a rule, they havea single large drainage hole. To avoid clogging, the holesare covered with large pieces of crock or other coarse ma-

SEQUENCE IN URNS.

ILLUSTRATION XII

Pink geraniums in one of the two black urns at the formal doorway of Mr. and Mrs. Houlder Hud-gins of Beacon Hill, Boston.

ILLUSTRATION XIII

The same urn in the fall with pyramidally trained English ivy.
Evergreen branches replace the ivy plants at Christmas time.

terial at planting time. Burlap and sphagnum moss are spread over this to prevent the soil from washing through.

Tin Cans

Gardeners in many places rely on tin cans. In sections of southern Europe, they are used almost exclusively; even oil drums are planted with trees. To improve their appearance, they are whitewashed or painted and either decorated with designs or covered with tiles. On Rhodes, I remember a yellow cottage with plant tins also painted yellow. In Piraeus, a little old woman grew grapes and pink hollyhocks in blue tin cans scattered over the rooftop and placed in front of her dazzling white house.

Plants thrive in tin cans because they hold moisture well. As in plastic pots, roots are distributed through the soil. One professional grower who experimented with geraniums in both tin and clay concluded that the cans gave superior results.

To make drainage holes in tins, use a hammer and a large nail or spike, punching from the inside out. This will bring the rough edges outside and not interfere with the outward flow of water. The larger the tins, the larger the outlets; with oil drums, make them with a crow bar. Set large tins on bricks or blocks of wood to allow water to pass freely through the drainage holes.

Plastic and Fiberglass Containers

Besides the smaller sizes, plastic pots are available in various shapes and forms, and in many colors. Indoor gardeners plant them with philodendrons, dracaenas, aloca-sias and other tropicals. In summer, the planters are taken out to shady terraces or porches where they perform double duty.

Also procurable are containers of other synthetic materials. One, a combination of fiberglass and plastic, known as

Fiberglas, is made into window boxes, room dividers, and liners for built-in plant boxes. If custom made, these cost more because they are hand moulded. They are obtainable in white, beige, slate gray, charcoal, turquoise, coral and other colors. Fiberglas containers are light, durable, and unaffected by cold. Nor do they corrode or conduct heat. The surface, which is soft and opaque, has a dull attractive luster that requires no refinishing. Non-porous and strong, a container weighing five pounds can hold 150 pounds of soil. In winter, plants suffer little damage from cold, but there is danger of flooding.

Rope and Basket Containers

Containers made of sisal rope (also used for boat rigging) are fine for seaside gardens. They are a burnishedbrown due to several coats of liquid plastic. Artistic in appearance, they are not harmed if left out through the winter.

In the garden, baskets give an Old World look and are effective near cedar or picket fences or on gates. Durable baskets hold soil for planting, but the lightweight types are only intended to cover unattractive tin cans or tar paper pots. Baskets also give weight to plastic pots and lessen the evaporation from clay containers.

Strawberry Barrels

The strawberry barrel is a delightful novelty for terrace or doorway. If you have not seen a wooden barrel with strawberries growing from openings at the sides, you may know the glazed strawberry jar, with strawberries, sedums, or strawberry begonias planted in the protruding cups.

5. SOIL MIXTURES AND PLANTING

To a great extent, the success of the container garden depends on proper soil. You can have good results with soil taken directly from the garden, but even better if you take time to prepare a proper mixture. This control of soil is where growing plants in containers has an advantage over gardening in the open ground.

Soil mixtures can also be purchased at nurseries and garden centers with special kinds available for acid-loving plants (azaleas, camellias, and gardenias) for ferns and begonias, and for cacti and other succulents. If you live in a city where garden soil is not easily obtainable or if you grow only a few plants, it is practical to buy a prepared mixture.

SOIL MIXTURES

A ll-Purpose

    2 parts good garden loam
    1 part sand
    1 part peat moss or leaf mold or other humus
    1 teaspoon bone meal for each 5-inch pot of mixture
    (5-inch potfull to each bushel)

For Acid-Lovers (Azaleas, Camellias, Gardenias, Heathers, etc.)
    2 parts good garden loam
    2 parts sand
    2 parts acid peat
    1 part leaf mold
    1/3 part old manure or 1/2 part dehydrated manure

For Fine-Root Plants (Begonias, Ferns, African Violets, Gloxinias, Christmas and Orchid Cacti, etc.)

2 parts good garden loam
2 parts sand
2 parts leaf mold or peat moss
½ part old manure or 1/2 part dehydrated manure

For Bulbs (Hyacinths, Daffodils, Tulips)

2 parts good garden loam
1 part sand
1 part leaf mold or peat moss
5 inch pot of bone meal for each bushel

For Cacti and Succulents

2 parts good garden loam
2 parts sand
½ part leaf mold or peat moss
5 inch pot of bone meal for each bushel
5 inch pot of finely ground limestone for each bushel

For Orchids and Bromeliads
6 parts Osmunda fiber
1 part of ½-inch charcoal

The container should be filled with $^1/_3$ drainage material. If Osmunda fiber is not available, use equal parts peat moss, sand and granulated charcoal.

PLANTING

When you are ready to mix ingredients, be sure the soil is damp and workable. To determine this, take a handful, squeeze it and allow it to drop. If water comes out, it is too wet; if it breaks apart, it is too dry. But if the lump of soil retains its shape or cracks just a little when it is dropped, it is in good condition to work.

Be certain containers are clean when you start. Soak used or new clay pots overnight so they will not drawmoisture from soil after planting. Clean dirty clay pots with a stiff brush and hot, soapy water.

Though redwood, cedar, and cypress containers may be left natural, they may also be stained or painted. First clean the surfaces then apply one or two coats of stain or paint. Let dry completely before planting. Concrete, metal, plastic, fiberglass, and similar materials all need cleaning.

Suit Plants to Containers

Consider the shape of each container, its color, and texture in relation to the color of flowers and foliage and the present as well as ultimate size of each plant. Don't choose material that is too small, and if you want a group of plants for a large container, select one tall specimen for the center to give height and scale.

In low pots or bulb pans and in tubs, use low-growing plants-fancy-leaved caladiums, petunias, verbenas, Ian-tanas, ageratum and wax begonias. Hyacinths, tulips, and daffodils are also appropriate. In tall containers, plant specimens of geraniums, heliotropes, coleus, balsam, dwarf dahlias, fuchsias, and marguerites. Reserve large tubs and boxes for trees and shrubs.

Keep in mind the form of plants, particularly the evergreens which stand out boldly in winter. Rounded types,as clipped yews or globe arborvitae, look well in angular containers. Hollies or yews, sheared into squares or pyramids, look better in circular tubs. This contrast of the curving with the straight always gives interest.

How to Pot

The first step in potting is to place sufficient drainage material in the bottom of each container so that water can pass through freely. An inch or two of flower pot pieces (rounded sides up), or chips of brick or flagstone, pebbles, gravel, small stones, or cinders can be used. The larger the container, the larger the pieces should be. Some gardeners spread a piece of coarse burlap and a layer of sand over large drainage pieces. A layer of Vermiculite or sphagnum moss over the drainage material is also fine to keep soil from clogging holes.

Above the drainage, spread a layer of soil, the amount depending on the size of the container and the root ball of the plant. Place the plant in position so that the surface of the soil will be an inch (more for big plants) below the rim of the container. This space is needed to hold water.

Fill soil in around the roots, firming gently with your fingers or a piece of wood so as to eliminate air pockets. Add more soil and firm, but do not make the soil too tightfor fine feeding roots must be able to penetrate it with ease.

Finally, water plants well, let them drain. If water passes through the pot very rapidly, press soil again to firm it. If the soil holds water too long, loosen it a little.

Place container plants in a sheltered spot out of sun and wind for the first week or so while they make new root growth and adjust to new conditions.

When your permanent trees, shrubs or perennials grow too large for their containers, shift them to bigger ones. Water the night before so the soil will be moist for transplanting. Dry soil tends to break apart, except on root-bound specimens. To remove most plants, invert the pot over your left hand and tap the pot rim sharply on a step or table or slip a knife around the inside edges. Turn larger plants on the side, knock the pot to loosen the plant and remove with a firm, gentle pull.

Handling Large Plants

Planting large specimens purchased in temporary containers is a more involved process. If they are in baskets or boxes, these can be broken or torn apart, but be careful not to disturb the roots. Tins must be opened with tin cutters. To remove plants, put the cut containers on their sides and pry steadily at the ball of soil gently in order not to break it.

All container plants benefit from a mulch spread evenly over the surface of the soil. This will keep the soil cool and moist and weeds under control. Use peat moss, sand, gravel, stones, pebbles, buckwheat hulls, or Vermiculite. One of these will also give an attractive appearance but since the mulch conceals the soil, it is more difficult to determine when to water. Test by poking a finger through the material to touch the soil.

Though drainage holes are recommended, they are not essential. I have seen flourishing geraniums and wax and tuberous begonias in jardinières, jugs, and iron kettles with only a thick layer of pebbles, broken flower pots, cinders, or coarse sand spread at the bottom to catch water. Of course, what is important here is a sensible program of watering rather than the presence or lack of drainage outlets.

Pointers for Planters

In the case of planters, again make certain drainage facilities are good. Usually there are holes at the base or sides. For best results, every four square feet should have a two-inch drainage outlet.

Planters attached to buildings are often open at thebase. As with other containers, before filling with soil, spread a thick layer of broken flower pots, crushed bricks or coarse gravel over the bottom. With large-sized planters, this should be six to eight inches thick with a layer of straw or sphagnum moss above to prevent soil washing. Planters require day-by-day care to keep plants at their best. This means pruning, staking, spraying, feeding, and more particularly watering. Planters adjoining walls dry out quickly, especially where heat is reflected from brick, stucco, or concrete. Often planters are located under overhanging roofs or broad eaves. Wherever they are, do not depend on rain, but apply the hose as often as needed, which is usually daily and sometimes more often. Remember to have planters in factories, offices, and public buildings watered on week-ends and through vacation periods.

Planting the Strawberry Barrel

You can make your own strawberry barrel from a nail keg (which is easy to handle) or a barrel. A 55-gallon molasses barrel is fine for your purpose.with a keg or barrel, first bore five or six half-inch holesin the bottom for drainage. Then make twoinch holes, inalternate rows, around the sides, starting six inches fromthe bottom. Keep the holes six to eight inches apart. Ifyou want the wood natural, treat it with a non-injurious preservative, or paint it with a light color to set off the foliage.

To enable all plants in the barrel to get water, insert a drainage pipe in the center. But first, spread broken crock or brick over the bottom with a two-inch layer of gravel on top. Then hold a piece of rolled cardboard upright in the center of the barrel and fill with sand. Or take a downspout, with several quarter-inch holes bored in the sides, and hold it in position in the center while you fill it with sand.

While holding the cylinder with one hand, with the other spread potting soil over the drainage layer and up to two inches from the lowest row of holes. Tamp to firm. Then add more soil just up to the holes. The cylinder should now stand alone while you insert plants through the holes. Spread out their roots and cover with soil.

Repeat to the top of the barrel, setting plants in the holes and tamping soil so it will not settle later. At the top, place more plants around the drainage cylinder, spacing them about six inches apart.

Pull out the cardboard when all the planting is finished. The sand will then act as a drainage outlet. However, if you used a perforated cylinder, let it stay. Then when you're watering your strawberry barrel, pour a little

water right into the cylinder to reach the plants at the base, and pour more over the top around the cylinder.

Besides fruiting strawberries, you can grow strawberry begonias, pick-a-back plants, episcias, chlorophytums, and small-leaved English ivies. When plants get rampant, remove some of the runners so the surface of the barrel will show a little. In hot, sunny positions, ivy-leaved geraniums, trailing lantanas, verbenas, cacti, and succulents will thrive. Annual sweet alyssum adapts itself well to this novelty container, and a combination of white, pink, and lavender varieties is a pleasant sight.

If you live where there is winter freezing, move the strawberry barrel to a cool, frost proof place. Alternating freezing and thawing is harmful, especially with the glazed jars, which crack and break. If you have a cool, well-lighted window for the barrel, plants can be left in place. Otherwise, you must remove them and plant again in the spring.

6. DAY-BY-DAY CARE FOR CONTAINER PLANTS

The container garden is really easy to care for. However, since plants are more prominently displayed than in the garden, they require regular attention to keep them looking their best. Enough water is most important.

To keep plants neat, remove faded flowers and yellow leaves as soon as they appear. If you go over your plants a little each day, it is easy to keep them well groomed. Some kinds, like fuchsias, drop old blossoms, which must be picked up by hand or with a small broom and dust pan. Also, keep sweeping up fallen leaves.

When geranium blossoms fade, remove them with a firm snap of the fingers or with pruning shears or scissors. Cut off faded petunias to prevent seed formation. Do the same for marigolds, verbenas, snapdragons, zinnias, stocks, and other annuals as well as hardy flowering trees and shrubs, tropical plants, perennials, and bulbs.

Pinch and Prune

Some plants need pinching to shape them and prevent legginess. Cut tips from English, German, and Kenilworth ivies, variegated vinca, and other trailing plants to make them short and bushy. This is more important with plants in containers on terraces and other paved surfaces. Also snip shoots of petunias, fuchsias, snapdragons, marigolds, browallia, and other annuals. Some perennials, like phlox and fall asters, remain shorter and produce smaller but more numerous flower heads if tips are pinched once or twice in the late spring or summer. This practice delays blooming, thus extending the flowering season.

Woody plants need regular pruning and clipping. With lemon, orange, oleander, Chinese hibiscus and other tender trees and shrubs, cut out dead branches and prune to open up and shape. Do the same with hardy, woody plants. For formal effects, shear yews, hollies, arborvitae, boxwood, pittosporum, and sweet bay after new growth has hardened. Jagged tips may be cut off at any time of the year.

Water With Care

The importance of proper watering cannot be stressed enough, since container plants that are exposed to wind and sun dry out quicker than those in the ground. There are no exact rules about watering. You have to become acquainted with the needs of various plants. The best way is to examine them daily and water when the surface of the soil begins to look dry. Feeling the soil will also help you determine moisture needs.

How much and when to water will depend on the kind of plant and soil, the type and size of container, and the amount of exposure to sun and wind. Climate and the weather also play their part. During hot spells, most plants need daily watering, except those in small clay pots, which may require it twice. Some plants, like fuchsias and tuberous begonias, wilt when dry, but geraniums and succulents are not so sensitive to neglect. On the other hand, it is good to let soil dry out a little between waterings. This prevents the soil from turning sour.

Since unglazed containers dry out quickest, watch them more closely. Wooden tubs, window boxes, and planters dry out more slowly; metal is the slowest of all. Groups of plants in large containers keep moist longer than single specimens. Groupings of plants, arranged close together, shade one another and help prevent excessive moisture loss.

ILLUSTRATION XIV *(upper left)*
Wheelbarrow with summer flowers on a front lawn. This novelty interests every passer-by.

ILLUSTRATION XV *(upper right)*
An old spinning wheel with a box of petunias in the front yard of Mrs. Beatrice Fredericks. Such unusual containers can often be found in attics and cellars.

ILLUSTRATION XVI *(lower left)*
Geraniums and vinca in boxes fastened to old farm wheels, an attraction on the lawn of a New England homestead.

ILLUSTRATION XVII *(lower right)*
Red geraniums and trailing vinca in an ornamental donkey cart on the lawn of Mr. and Mrs. William L. O'Brien.

Ways to Water

There are several methods of watering. If you have many containers or large ones, depend on the hose, allowing water to flow through slowly and gently. Water small pots with a watering can that has a long spout. When plants are grouped closely, set up a sprinkler or hose with a fine spray nearby, allowing it to run for a long while, until soil is soaked. In California, where large containers are common and where summers are dry, a permanent apparatus is often set up for watering trees and shrubs and flowering plants with just the turn of a faucet. With geraniums and petunias, avoid sprinklers which spot blossoms.

One thing is certain; you must not depend on rain. Even heavy showers deposit a surprisingly small amount of moisture, and unless rains are frequent and lengthy, you must do your own watering. Window boxes and other containers near houses or under trees can stay dry in spite of an all-day downpour.

Though it is essential to give enough water, it is equally important not to overwater and so cause root rot. Over-watering also prevents aeration of the soil, and causes it to turn sour.
One good method is to set containers, if not too large,in a basin or pail of water for several hours, or until the surface of the soil feels moist. Or immerse the pot in a tub or large barrel of water and leave it there until air is eliminated and the

bubbling stops.The best general rule is to soak soil thoroughly when you water and then allow it to go just a bit dry before you water again.

Vacation Time

If you go away for long periods during the summer, give the container garden serious thought before making it a project. On the other hand, you can enjoy both holidays and plants if you are absent for only short periods. The best safeguard is to entrust your plants to a responsible friend. Some neighborhoods employ handy men for this, as does Beacon Hill in Boston for its extensive window-box project. Landscape gardeners will come to water, as will nurserymen, who have more time for this during the quieter months of summer.

Several devices can be practiced. One is to arrange smaller containers in boxes of peat moss, sawdust, or soil, which has been well soaked. Then there is the pot-in-pot method, whereby small pots are set in larger ones, with moist peat moss inserted between. Some enthusiasts even take their plants with them when they are vacationing.

Move Plants About

Every now and then you will want to shift plants around to accommodate their needs. On hot, windy days, move into the shade exposed pots that are subjected to reflected heat from stone walls, concrete walks, or paved areas. Remember, too, that hanging baskets dry out the quickest. In the event of a violent wind or rain storm, move containers to safety.

Fertilizer

A good feeding program will result in healthier plants with more bloom. In the confined soil areas of containers, plants utilize nutrients sooner than they do in the garden; so, in general, feed plants every two weeks with a balanced chemical fertilizer, following directions on the package, for more immediate results, apply liquid fertilizer. Some plants are voracious and will need more frequent feeding. Foliar fertilizer can be applied as a supplement.

Saucers

Containers on pavements, patios, walks and driveways will not need saucers and are better without them, for water will run out freely. However, on other surfaces, as painted porch floors or tables, saucers are needed to prevent staining. You can use plastic saucers, light, non-breakable and inexpensive, in black, gray, green, rose, or red. Avoid clay saucers, since their penetrating moisture leaves circular, whitish marks. When saucers are used, be careful that pots do not stand in leftover water for any length of time.

From time to time, clean saucers with a stiff brush and soapy water. Containers will also require washing out. Painted tubs that stand on or near plant beds become spattered with mud during heavy rains or during sprinkling. If the mud is allowed to dry, it will rub off easily with a piece of cloth or your fingers. When you plan a party, it is a good idea to give containers a quick going-over with a damp cloth or sponge to make them sparkle.

When to Repot

As plants become pot bound, they will need shifting to larger quarters. This applies to such permanent plants as trees and shrubs, but not to annuals or temporary kinds. Though spring and fall are the best times to repot, it can be done any time if roots are not disturbed. Usually, the rule is to move a plant to a container of the next larger size. If a plant is in an eight- or nine-inch pot, shift to a ten-inch size. If it is already in a ten-inch size, supply a tub that is just an inch or two wider in diameter.

As a rule, tub bed trees and shrubs can stay in the same container for several years if fed regularly and if some soil is removed from the top annually and replaced with fresh mixture. Some actively growing plants may require moving to large containers every two years. On the whole, avoid overlarge containers since the soil will hold too much moisture for plants to absorb it quickly. Overpot-ting tends to promote a water-logged condition.

Winter Care

Winter care varies with climate and types of plants. Discard annual and temporary kinds and bring house plants indoors or to a greenhouse. Palms, gardenias, and camellias in the South and yews, arborvitae, and pieris in the North can be left outdoors. In some cases, they will require shifting to less exposed spots and may even need covering with burlap, plastic film, or evergreen branches to guard against windburn or sunscald. Spraying the tops of evergreens with plastic wax in the early winter will cut down on evaporation. Remember that container plants in the winter still need water, but if soil freezes hard, wait for periods of thaw.

Where temperature drops to zero and below, soil will freeze solidly and many hardy plants may be killed. This is due, not so much to cold, but to frozen soil, which doesnot allow tops to draw moisture, though they are still constantly transpiring. In below-zero regions, hardy evergreens, arborvitae, Japanese yew, hemlock, pines, and Douglas fir, if planted in containers with sufficient soil, will survive winters out of doors.

Where temperatures drop only to twenty degrees above, the choice of plant material is greater, extending to pieris, rhododendrons, azaleas, false cypress, firs, English and Korean boxwoods, cherry laurel, leucothoe, mahonia, and climbing euonymus. English ivy, myrtle, and pachysan-dra are three low evergreens that are reliably hardy. For milder climates, with little or no freezing, the choice is almost limitless, including camellias, oleander, hibiscus, crotons, poinsettia, aucuba, pittosporum, nandina, podo-carpus, acacias, palms, bougainvillea, and ficus, not to mention many annuals.

In sections where soil does not freeze, watering is no problem in winter. Unless rains are frequent, water with the hose, sprinkler, or watering can. Depending on climate, sweet bay, oleander, orange and lemon trees will need the winter protection of a cool greenhouse, a well-lighted shed or unheated room where above-freezing temperatures can be maintained. During this resting period, give just enough water to prevent soil from drying out.

Winter Preparation \or Spring

The winter, too, is the time to clean and prepare con tainers for the next season. Bring indoors-into cellar shed, tool house, garage, attic, or spare room-easily moved containers, as this will help preserve them. Espe cially is this true of materials that deteriorate, among them several kinds of wood. Clay or glazed pots will break if not emptied of soil, which freezes and thaws, creating pressure against the sides. Valuable glazed or porcelain containers should never be left outdoors, with or without soil.

Empty soil from clay pots before bringing them in and then clean them with a stiff brush and hot water plus a detergent. Empty the soil from wooden tubs and boxes as well and scrub surfaces with soap and water. Paint or stain them later when they are thoroughly dry. Plant stands, wall brackets, baskets, wooden hanging baskets, small window boxes and other containers should be cleaned late in fall and made ready for the coming season well before planting time in spring.

Large planters, boxes, and window boxes, which are not easy to move, must be left outdoors. However, their condition should be carefully checked before winter sets in to see whether they need bracing or a coat of paint.

7. GERANIUMS GALORE

All over the country, geraniums flaunt their red and scarlet, rose, pink, and white blooms with a gay abandon that few other plants can rival. In boxes on city fire escapes and rooftops, in window boxes on surburban and country houses, in tubs and pots on terraces and patios, and in hanging baskets of the porches of summer cottages, they are beloved and cherished plants-a welcome symbol of warmth and hospitality. For sheer impact of color, they cannot be surpassed.

Geraniums are also great favorites in Europe, where red- and pink-flowering zonals, the common types, are commonly treated as bedding plants. In western and northern European countries, they are widely planted in window boxes and in pots and tubs at doorways of city and country gardens. Along the Mediterranean, where geraniums are hardy, zonal types develop into mounds that are six feet tall and equally broad. Ivy-leaved kinds clothe banks and slopes and cascade like waterfalls from balconies, rooftops, and garden walls.

This widespread planting is easy to understand. Notonly is the geranium a spectacular flower, but it grow; almost everywhere with ease, blossoming under neglect and surviving where other plants fail. Though it prefer: and needs sun to bloom, it tolerates shade, where it is usually handled as a foliage plant. What it resents is toe much moisture and a rich diet. Kept too wet, the leave; turn yellow; given a heavy soil, one high in nitrogen plants go to foliage and flower sparingly.

Even at that geraniums are amazing plants that will perform admir ably under a wide variety of growing conditions.

Actually, the name geranium is incorrect, for these free flowering shrubby plants are members of the genus *Pelar gonium*. The Greek word, meaning stork-bill, refers to the slender, curving form of the seed pod. Nevertheless geranium is the commonly used name for the members of this interesting clan.

GREAT VARIETY OF TYPES

Far from uniform, the genus includes types that are herbaceous, shrubby, deciduous, annual, biennial, perennial, stem less, long-stemmed, tuberous and fibrous-rooted -all of them well suited to container gardening. Even if you choose no other plants, you could have a varied pot garden of single and double zonal, fancy-leaved or variegated, scented-leaved, ivy and Lady or Martha Washington geraniums (also called show or fancy geraniums), not to mention a few oddities of cactus and climbing types.

Zonal, Fancy- and Scented-leaved

The zonal geranium is characterized by dark circular markings on the rounded green leaves. Double types dominate the trade and are offered by florists in the spring for planting in gardens and window boxes. You will like such pinks as Mrs. Lawrence, Fiat Enchantress, and Pink Abundance. Olympic Red is excellent, as is Better Times, an outstanding dark crimson. Among desirable singles, consider the carmine Barbara Hope, the cherry-red to white Apple Blossom, the creamy coral Ecstasy, the scarlet to wine-red Nuit Poitevine, and the light orchid-pink Helen Van Pelt Wilson. All are so beautiful, they should be planted where they can easily be seen.

Variegated geraniums, with leaves that are often brilliantly colored, are attractive even out of bloom. Indeed, some feel, as I do, that flowers detract from the foliage. Among the best are

Mrs. Cox, vermillion and purple, with an edging of yellow; Miss Burdett Coutts, purple-zoned and pink-splashed; and Skies of Italy, crimson-zoned with a yellow edging. Set among green-leaved geraniums and other foliage plants, pots of the variegateds add color and pattern.

ILLUSTRATION XVIII
Ceramic woven basket with pink ivy-leaved geraniums in the garden of Mr. and Mrs. Theodore B. Griffith.

Scented-leaved geraniums comprise a varied group that is treasured for the scent of the crushed leaves. The flowers, smaller and less showy than those of zonal, are not so important. Familiar kinds include the nutmeg, with round leaves and small white flowers; the peppermint, with large, hairy, velvety leaves; the pine-scented, with big finely-cut leaves; the rose, with deeply-cut, toothed leaves; and the lemon-scented, with small leaves on compact plants. A variety of the lemon-scented, Prince Rupert, is admired for its variegated green-and-white leaves. Scented-leaved geraniums prefer a light, well-drained loam. They make unique pot plants, and for a black iron kettle nothing is more decorative than a great sprawling peppermint geranium.

Ivy-leaved and Lady Washington Types

The trailing, ivy-leaved geraniums are among the most profuse flowering when grown under favorable conditions. They dislike shade and high humidity and thrive best in climates with warm days and cool nights, as in California. In window boxes, they offer a pleasant change from English ivy and vinca and present masses of lively color in hanging baskets suspended on porches, posts, lath houses, garages, or trees. Adaptable basket varietiesinclude the lilac-white to pink Alliance, the double pint Galilee, and the lavender Santa Paula.

Lady Washington's, considered the handsomest of ge raniums, are not so easy to grow. Like the ivy-leaved, the) prefer cool nights and warm, sunny days, responding tc shelter from wind and all-day sun. You may want a few for variety's sake, like the lovely Easter Greeting, Lucy Becker, Gay Nineties, and Marie Rober. Lady Washington geraniums are sold by florists at Easter time, and gift plants you receive can be included in the container garden.

Cactus and Climbing

If you are a geranium enthusiast, you may want to spark your pot plant collection with some cactus and climbing geraniums. They have bizarre and fascinating forms and flowers and are certain to arouse comment. There is the parsley-leaved Otidia, the heart-leaved, knotted and rue-scented stork-bills, the prickly-stalked geranium, and the climbing square-stalked Jenkinsonia. Perhaps they are more interesting than handsome.

Sunshine Required

Geraniums are sun-loving plants. They will grow in window boxes and pots on the east, south, or west side of the house and on terraces with sun for half a day. In spite of their love of sunshine, they will even flourish with just a little, provided they receive plenty of strong light. The north side of a house, beyond the shade of trees, will produce extraordinary plants. When geraniums are grown against hot, sunny brick, concrete, or stone walls or pavements, some shielding from the torrid noonday sun is advisable. This is to cut down on reflected heat through the middle part of the day.

Soil and Potting

Geraniums flourish and look well in pots, boxes, and planters. They thrive in various soil mixtures if drainage is good. For abundant bloom, however, supply a special preparation, not high in nitrogen, or lush foliage and few blooms will result. A combination of three parts good garden loam and one part leaf mold, peat moss, or compost plus a five-inch pot of bone meal to each bushel is good. If the garden loam is heavy, add sand. Acid soil will also need some lime. I have success with good garden soil and a sprinkling of a 5-10-5 fertilizer and bone meal. During the growing season, plants respond to a low-nitrogen fertilizer in liquid form.

When potting, be generous with drainage material to insure free passage of water. Always water with care, sincetoo much or not enough can be harmful. The best rule is to water when the surface of the soil feels dry. Then soak the soil well and do not water again until plants need it. If soil is kept too wet, leaves will turn yellow; if too dry they wilt and discolor. Both extremes cause legginess, a common complaint from gardeners.

Keep up Appearance

To maintain even plant growth, turn containers frorr time to time. Remove yellow leaves and faded blossoms which are especially distracting on plants at doorways anc other key spots. If rain rots and disfigures the centei florets of the heads, pull them off with your fingers, leav ing the unmarred outer florets and buds. This is admittedly an exacting chore for the busy gardener, but one that greatly improves the appearance of plants.

On the whole, geraniums are pest free, but if insects prove troublesome, malathion or lindane will clean them up. To your delight, you may even discover dead Japanese beetles on the foliage, since flower and leaf parts contain a substance that is poisonous to this pest.

Winter Care

If you want plants for next spring, take two- to four-inch cuttings in August or early September. Look for

ILLUSTRATION XIX

Tree trunk with a tin of geraniums at the driveway entrance of the estate of the late Alvin T. Fuller. Trunks cut directly to the ground also provide appropriate settings for container plants mature stems (with leaves spaced close together) tha break easily like a snap bean. Woody growth is hard to root and succulent tips tend to rot. Before planting spread out cuttings in a shady place for several hours sc leaves will lose excess moisture.

Rooting Cuttings

When ready to plant, cut off the lower leaves, allowing but two or three to each cutting. Also pull off the little wings on the stem, since they are inclined to rot. Dip stem ends in hydrated lime to prevent decay and then insert about halfway, in a flat or large pot of pure sand or a mix ture of sand and peat moss. With geraniums, rooting powders are hardly necessary. When cuttings develop inch-long roots, they are ready for spacing out in another flat or for separate planting in 2½-inch pots. Fill with *a* mixture of three parts sandy loam and one part peat moss or leaf mold. After planting, keep in the shade for the first few days, and bring indoors before cold weather.

When the separated cuttings have developed strong root systems, shift to 3½- or 4-inch pots. Use the same potting mixture as before, with bone meal added. Later as established plants begin to grow, feed periodically with a high phosphorous fertilizer, as 5-10-5 or 4-12-8.

To keep plants bushy and to encourage branching inch while small, starting when they are three to four inches high. Provide sunny windows, and keep turning pots to prevent lopsided growth. Water regularly, but allow soil to dry out just a little between applications. Above all, do not permit pots to stand in water, but set them on pebbles spread out in the saucers. Best growing temperatures are 60 to 70 degrees F. by day, no higher, with a ten degree drop at night, though this is not always possible in the average home.

If you wish, you can hold onto your original plants and winter them indoors. Cut back tops to 6 or 8 inches, and if containers are not too enormous, place them in a sunny house or a well-lighted cellar window. The important thing in winter is to grow old plants cool, at about 50 degrees F., and to water sparingly to encourage rest.

Plants may also be wintered in cool cellars with little light. Remember only that the less light, the cooler the temperatures should be. This is because too much warmth and insufficient light cause lanky growth that undermines vigor.

In late winter or early spring, if old plants are growing in strong light, take cuttings for young plants to use outdoors, rooting by the method described. Or if you prefer, when weather permits, cut back your old plants, repot them in fresh soil and set outdoors. Many gardeners findthis method successful, and it does provide big specimens Growers of geraniums often ask whether plants can be lifted in fall and stored by hanging upside down in cellar or basements. This was possible in old-fashioned cellar with dirt floors and without central heating units; but it is not possible in modern basements, which are warm, dry and well insulated. Gardeners with cellars or sheds when temperatures remain above freezing, can winter gera niums this way. The dead-looking sticks, set out in pots or in the garden in warm weather, will astound you when they develop into glorious flowering specimens. The fact that geraniums, under certain conditions, can be wintered without soil is certainly proof of their toughness.

8. TUBEROUS BEGONIAS IN SHADE

For large, brilliant blooms in open shade or filtered sunlight, tuberous begonias, in their varied forms and colors, can be the answer to your need. Today these gorgeous flowering bulbs are enjoying tremendous popularity, and some amateur gardeners collect them, as they do geraniums, fuchsias, and dahlias, or African violets indoors. Hybrid varieties, far removed from the original species, are truly exotic beauties which are easy and rewarding to grow. They solve the problem of what to consider for part shade, particularly where vivid colors are needed to enliven terraces or porches.

Tuberous begonias are classified according to shape of bloom-camellia-flowered, including the picotee or double marginata; carnation flowered; single-frilled or crispa, including *Begonia crispa marginata;* hanging basket; crested; rosebud; *B. multiflora;* daffodil-flowered; and hollyhock-flowered.

The camellia-flowered begonias are very popular. Older varieties, with their smooth margins, did not resemble camellias as much as the newer hybrids, with their ruffled, wavy-edged petals. In the picotee or double mai ginata class, the edges are of contrasting color and th broad border is usually irregular. They make lovely pot plants.

The carnation-flowered begonias produce smaller, gen- erally heavier blooms in an extensive color range. The lovely single-frilled or crispa begonias have ruffled petals In one form, *Begonia crispa marginata,* the edges offer color contrast. Fascination is a delightful variety in this group.

For Hanging Baskets, Planters, and Window Boxes

Hanging-basket tuberous begonias, the cascading types *B. pendula flora-plena,* bear single or double blooms or arching stems. As a rule, these smaller-flowering types an more floriferous than the large ones. There is also a strair that produces miniature camellia-like flowers.

Crested begonias, *B. cristata*, have slightly frilled single flowers. These are carried above the foliage. One of the loveliest is Autumn Glow, with apricot flowers crested with dark copper, handsome as an accent plant in a con tainer.

The interesting rosebud types, in shades of rose andpink, are favorites with many gardeners, though the flowers tend to develop poor centers when they mature. Plants have a free-flowering habit.

Begonia multiflora is the small-flowered type sometimes listed as nana. Well known and still one of the best is the yellow Madame Helene Harms. On plants to six inches tall, multiflora begonias support flowers high above the foliage. Their compact habit and free-flowering nature make them good for large planters. Excellent, too, for window boxes, they withstand more heat and direct sunshine than the others, especially along coastal areas where fogs prevail.

Daffodil-flowered begonias, represented by a few varieties, are grown chiefly as oddities, especially by collectors. They are interesting specimen plants to include in a group.

The hollyhock-flowered begonia, *B. martiana*, is another novelty, with flowers close to the stem. In sun, plants attain two feet, but under lath or in partial shade, they may grow to four feet. The two-inch single blossoms are light pink, darker in sun. This begonia can be grown for background or accent among a group of potted plants or in a wide planter.

A Hardy Begonia

Another tuberous begonia is the so-called hardy type *B. evansiana,* which survives winters on Long Island and is hardy from Philadelphia southward. Two-foot plant have handsome pointed leaves, a branching habit, and an abundance of single, light pink flowers. Stems are a con trasting rosy-red, and there is a white form. Several pots o the hardy begonia at the doorway or in a sheltered corner can be a choice item in the container garden.

Maine Success Story

Certainly, tuberous begonias are well adapted to con tainer culture. One enthusiast, Malcolm Cox of Round Pond, Maine, who has been growing prize-winning plant for over thirty years, plants his more than 200 tubers in individual pots and window boxes. He finds that potted plants, arranged in tiers in front of his white colonial house, can be seen better when raised, since the heavy blooms are inclined to face downward. Furthermore when grown in the ground, they tend to become spattered by rain or by the garden hose. Mr. Cox prepares a special soil for his begonias-two parts light garden soil, one part old cow manure, one part peat moss, plus a five-inch pot of bone meal to a wheelbarrow of mixture. In containershis begonias are protected by high branching trees that cast filtered shade.

Start Them Indoors

Because of the short growing season in the North, tuberous begonias need an early indoor start to insure bloom by midsummer. Even where the growing period is longer, it is best to start tubers in pots or trays some time between February and April. Tubers can be planted in flats or bulb pans (low pots) in a mixture of equal parts clean sand and peat moss. Set them with the hollow side up, for this is the top. Barely cover the tubers with the soil mixture and arrange them just an inch or two apart, since they will remain in these flats but a short time. Water sparingly, but do not allow to dry out. A temperature of

70 to 75 degrees F. is fine; if it is cooler, growth will be delayed considerably and you will lose time. Until sprouts appear, light is not necessary, but after that, give full light to insure compact growth. East or west windows are good, but a small greenhouse is even better.

Room for Growth

After the sprouts are an inch or two high, transplant tubers to roomier quarters. They may be well spaced in large flats, but individual four-inch pots are better because roots will not be disturbed when plants are shifted later. You may even take a short cut now and move them to the final containers.

The size of the permanent containers will depend or the size of the tubers. If they are two inches in diameter they will need six-inch pots. Give three-inch bulbs eight inch pots, a size well suited to large plants. Because glazed pots and wooden containers stay moist longer and do not accumulate mosses and fungi, they are ideal. In window boxes, space plants five to six inches apart, keeping taller kinds in the back and pendulous or multiflora (nana) varieties along the front.

To grow well, sprouted tubers need a special potting mixture-equal parts good garden soil, leaf mold or peat moss, old manure (or a small amount of dehydrated), plus sand for drainage. If the plants are in small pots, use this mixture when transferring them to larger pots. When frost danger is over, plants can go outdoors, but shade them for the first week.

Need for Sun and Food

Finally, wherever you place containers, be certain plants receive filtered or light sunshine for about three hours a day, preferably early or late in the day, when rays are not so hot. Many gardeners misinterpret shade tomean the dense shade of low-branching trees. Here, most plants do very poorly. Open shade on the north sides of houses, and filtered and checkered shade through a lacy network of high branching trees offers an ideal environment for these plants. In cooler climates they can tolerate more direct sunlight.

Tuberous begonias are heavy feeders. Even when you prepare the soil richly, plants will need more sustenance through the growing period. Apply liquid fertilizer, according to directions, while plants are growing actively or topdress wth dry manure about every three weeks. But also keep in mind that too much fertilizer can burn foliage and cause bud drop. To send strength into root and leaf development, cut off the first bud while it is rather small (but not if you are anxious for early flowers). After blooming starts, nip off the two small female flowers on each side of the large, showy male blossoms. This will increase their size.

Keep Moist but Not Wet

Always keep plants moist, but not wet. Usually, watering once a day is sufficient, but this will depend on the type and size of containers, their placement, and the weather. Move plants around until you find places wherethey grow best. Also turn them to prevent one-sided de velopment.

As plants get tall, they will need support for the heavy blooms. When inserting stakes, be careful not to strike the tubers, and use raffia or soft twine to secure the tender stems. In some cases, extra large blooms will need indi vidual tying, and there are specially cushioned support! of English make for this purpose. From time to time syringe foliage, preferably in late afternoon or early eve ning so it will dry before dark. Avoid sprinkling, however, in moist, foggy climates where mildew can be a problem,

Mealy bugs, white flies, leaf hoppers, and aphids can all be checked with lindane or malathion. For thrips, apply DDT or lindane. Use a poison bait with metaldehyde base for snails or slugs and Bordeaux mixture for bacterial leaf spot. In mildew areas, apply captan or the newer karathane as a precaution. These problems, however, are rather uncommon, and very likely you will not be bothered by any of them.

To Store Tubers in Winter

Tubers can be held over from year to year if storedproperly during the winter. In fall in cold areas, frosts will blacken the foliage, but in warmer regions the needfor rest will be indicated by yellowing without actualfrost. Usually this occurs in October, when it is advisable to withhold water. After frost kills tops or they turn yellow, lift plants carefully with a spading fork so as not to injure them. Then, with the tops attached, spread the tubers in the sun for a few hours to dry. After the drying period, cut off tops; but if a portion of stem remains, do not break off. Allow it to dry before removing it later.

Finally, shake off the soil, arrange tubers in trays or shallow boxes, and cover with dry peat moss or clean, dry sand. The ideal storage temperatures is 45 to 50 degrees F. Some gardeners winter the clean tubers in paper bags, keeping the same colors together, and results are just as good. You can also leave tubers in pots. In this case, simply turn containers on sides and store in cellar, basement, shed or other frost proof spot where temperatures remain 40 to 60 degrees F. If kept too warm, bulbs tend to shrivel and their future as handsome pot plants for locations in filtered sunlight is seriously jeopardized.

9. THE SPLENDID FUCHSIAS

If you want enchanting flowering plants for shade, rely on the fuchsias. Whether in individual pots, window boxes, or hanging baskets, lady's ear drops, as fuchsias an sometimes called, are gorgeous plants noted for their grace and splendor. There are hundreds of varieties, sin gle and double, in rose, purple, and white shades, and in both upright and hanging types. Fuchsias are particularly popular in California, where the summers are cool and the winters sufficiently moderate; but they make handsome container plants in other climates too.

Except for the hanging types, fuchsias are by nature upright shrubby growers, fine as specimen plants for containers. Under proper conditions, some attain considerable size. The dark purple-and-red Reiter's Giant grows to five feet or more, and the single red Mephisto is even taller. Alice Hoffman, a semi-double white and pink, is a dwarf, to two feet, as is the three-foot Camellia, a double white and red.

Tree Types

Tree, or standard, fuchsias are always greatly admired. These are simply the usual fuchsias trained to tree form. With patience, you can develop your own, starting with a four- to five-inch cutting kept tied to a strong four- to five-foot stake. At the desired height of two, three, or four feet, the single stalk can be pinched back and allowed to branch. In the meantime, do not remove all leaves from the stem, because they are needed to manufacture food.

Good varieties to train to tree form include the purple-and-red Muriel, the red-and-white Storm King, the double lavender-and-red Gypsy Queen, and the all-white Flying Cloud. Tree fuchsias lend themselves to the simplicity of modern architecture; the large specimens are always attractive on the terraces and patios of contemporary ranch houses. On the other hand, they are also handsome with houses and gardens of traditional design.

For Hanging Baskets

Many gardeners believe that the best way to appreciate fuchsias is in hanging baskets, because their exquisite blooms are seen at or above eye level. They are most decorative for patios, entrances, lath houses, and on walls and tree trunks. They can be suspended in redwood slat boxesand in glazed or plastic containers. In moss-lined wire baskets, they require more water because the roots dry out more quickly.

For basket planting, you will like the double magenta-and-carmine Anna, the single red-and-white Claret Cup, and also the semi-double purple-and-red Muriel, mentioned for tree-training. Among the most brilliant varieties are the double, bright red Marinka; the nearly orange Aurora Superba; the carmine-rose and orange-red San Francisco; and the rose-purple-and-pink Amapola. It is more effective to grow but one variety in a container.

Espaliers and Pyramids

In planters or raised beds of containers, fuchsias can be trained into interesting espalier forms against a wall or fence where the space may be too narrow for other plants. Though not difficult, the espalier plant requires time and patience. First make a trellis of wood or wire. Five to seven tiers are customary. Then train your plant as it grows, pinching growth frequently to induce branching and to avoid bare stems. Varieties to espalier include the red-and-scarlet Falling Stars, the blue-and-rose Coquette, and the red-and-white Dr. John Gallwey.

Fuchsias can also be trained into pyramids in the manner of formal English ivy plants. Since the young fuchsia shoots tend to break easily, it takes patience and a steady hand to tie them properly to the form. Fully grown plants are delightful in a formal setting, and a pair for an en-tranceway are distinctive indeed.

Basic Needs

These tender woody plants do best under cool, humid conditions. They are especially successful in coastal areas, where fog and humidity prevail, though some varieties, as the single all-red Mephisto and the red-and-white Mme. Cornelissen, will thrive in hot, dry inland regions. They are great favorites because they bloom in shade, not the heavy shade of low-branching trees, but high, open shade and that found on the north side of a building. In dense shade, plants get leggy and flower sparingly. In hot, direct sunshine, however, they dry out and the leaves burn. In hot climates, lath houses provide ideal conditions. Windy locations should be avoided because of the delicate flowers and brittle branches.

Moisture is essential. Plants announce dryness by wilting. In containers, they usually need water every day and sometimes more often. Good drainage is important. In the bottom of the container provide sufficient rough material-broken flower pots, pebbles, or cinders-to insure free passage of water. Do not allow pots to stand in water,and in hot weather sprinkle the foliage to remove dust and increase humidity.

Fuchsias require an acid soil. The mixture must be rich in organic matter. A good combination consists of one part good garden loam, one part leaf mold or peat moss, and either one part old manure or a small amount in dehydrated form.

Containers should be large enough to allow for full development of plants during the summer growing season. A small plant needs a six-inch pot; if two or three are grown together, use a ten- or twelve-inch pot. Starting with young plants is preferable, although large specimens are satisfactory if they are healthy and vigorous. When fuchsias are wintered in containers and are not treated as annuals, you can enrich the growing medium the first year by scooping a few inches of soil from the top and replacing it with a fresh mixture. The next year, take plants out of containers in early spring, cut back the tops and some of the roots and repot in fresh soil in the same container. Drastically cutting back branches in the spring, before growth commences, will make plants branch well.

Increasing Your Supply

When you want to increase your collection, take three-inch cuttings from the tender spring growth, dip the ends in a hormone powder and insert the lower inch of each stem in a mixture of half leaf mold and half sand. Protect the cuttings from sun and either spray them lightly from time to time or cover with polyethylene plastic to prevent their drying out. When roots have formed, transfer the plants to small pots in a mixture of light loam and leaf mold. Cuttings can also be taken in late summer or early fall for small plants that are easier to winter.

Voracious in their needs, fuchsias require regular feeding through the growing season. Give liquid fertilizer once a month, following directions on the package. Fish emulsion, applied monthly, will give especially good results.

During the winter, store plants at 45 to 50 degrees to keep them dormant. Water sparingly, just enough to prevent wood from shriveling. Outdoors, hardy fuchsias will survive to 25 degrees, but where hardiness is questionable, it is safer to winter plants in a greenhouse, cool room, shed, or in a cold frame. During this period, cover the roots with a layer of peat moss.

Insects likely to attack fuchsias include aphids, red spiders, white flies, thrips, mealy bugs, and leaf hoppers. Malathion, lindane, or DDT applied regularly, especially before an infestation is heavy, will keep these enemies under control.

10. PETUNIAS AND OTHER FINE ANNUALS

Petunias are indispensable for the container garden. Gay and colorful, easy to grow, free-flowering, available in a variety of types, and generally free of problems, they are really a wonderful annual. If you have space for but one flowering plant, by all means choose petunias. Grow them from seed or buy young seedlings in flats in spring. Either way, you will have quick, satisfying results.

Rewarding Plants

The merits of petunias are worth elaborating, though they are well known. If it is bright splashes of color you want, red, pink, and rose petunias are the answer. Yet they come in blues and purples, as well as pure white, with some varieties producing individual blooms that are several inches across. The flowering period is always a long one, and plants that start blooming in May will continue into September and October, even into November. In the warmest areas of the country, they are grown for winter bloom. Other annuals look tired at the end of the season, but not petunias. In the autumn, they hold their own with the chrysanthemums. Even if you do not keep snipping off old blossoms and seed pods, a job really worth doing, plants will continue their exuberant performance.

Adaptability to many situations has made the petunia a popular summer flower everywhere. Luxuriating in full sun, it will bloom freely if given sun for a few hours a day and will also tolerate partial shade. Not fussy about soil, petunia will flourish in poor soil. It is also one of the few annuals that will flower satisfactorily in soil too rich for other kinds.

78

In recent years, breeders have developed useful types-balcony petunias for window boxes, as well as forms that are single, frilled, or double. The extensive color range includes red, rose, pink, salmon, blue, lavender, purple, pale yellow and white.

Types of Petunias

Petunias are divided into several groups, including singles and doubles and according to growth habit, type of bloom, and use. Outstanding for their vigor, florifer-ousness, and uniformity of growth are the multiflora hybrids-the red Comanche, rosy-salmon Linda, salmon Silver Medal, white Paleface, and red-and-white-stripedGlitters. Equally remarkable are the grandiflora fringed hybrids like deep salmon Ballerina, salmon-pink May-time, deep scarlet-salmon Tango, rose-pink-on-white Crusades, and the white but yellow throated La Paloma.

Doubles include such favorites as the rose-with-white Gaiety, scarlet Allegro, rose-pink Caprice, scarlet Mrs. Dwight D. Eisenhower, rosy purple Rhapsody, and white Sonata. In large boxes, where bedding effects are desired, grow the nana compacta, or dwarf compact petunias. The bright blue Admiral, deep salmon Cheerful, red Fire-chief, pink Rosy Morn and the yellow-throated White Perfection are some in this classification.

For small containers or the edging of boxes and planters, choose the miniatures-the rosy Bright Eyes with a white throat, rose-starred white Twinkles, light Silvery Blue, and white Igloo. For hanging baskets, window boxes, shelves, and wall brackets, there is nothing prettier than the balcony types with their cascading habit. In this group are the mahogany Black Prince, deep Royal Blue, and clear Royal Rose.

Try petunias, too, in pots and tubs, boxes and movable planters. Window boxes and small planters on driveways, walks, terraces and porches offer excellent settings for their summer cheer. Since they are easy to raise from seed and inexpensive to buy as seedlings, keep extra petunias on hand to replace other plants that pass their prime in the planters attached to the house. Petunias are ideal for window boxes with emphasis on one variety. Alone the frilled rose-pink Prima Donna or the red Co-manche will give a striking effect.

Companionable Flowers

Petunias combine well with geraniums, heliotropes, lobelias, sweet alyssum, dwarf marigolds, patient Lucy, coleus, vinca, and German ivy. Some gardeners dislike petunias with the distracting foliage of coleus, but plain white petunias with red- or pink-leaved coleus make a pleasing picture. In front of evergreens, the colors of petunias seem more intense, a good reason for using them with yews, junipers, boxwood, and hollies in large planters.

In containers petunias can be planted six to eight inches apart, closer than in the garden. For their more confined roots, the soil mixture should be well prepared, with bone meal or super phosphate added. If soil is heavy, lighten it with sand or peat moss. This will also make it porous. When feeding during the growing season, use a high phosphorous combination-5-10-5 or 2-6-2. Plants will need sun for several hours a day if you expect bountiful results.

Pinch Periodically

When plants are a few inches high, pinch out tips to encourage branching, and as they grow keep pinching to keep plants compact. If you snip the first blossom, the plants will flower more profusely. Remove faded blooms each day or at least twice a week to improve the plant's appearance and prevent seed formation.

Water petunias when they need it, usually when the surface of the soil looks dry. Allowed to dry out completely, plants will wither, yet with too much water they may rot. Apply fertilizer, preferably in liquid form, every three to four weeks, one teaspoon of a balanced type to one gallon of water.

Heavy rains will spoil blooms. If possible, move containers to shelter. Avoid watering plants with sprinkler or hose, for water spots petals, particularly the dark purple varieties. New blooms, however, replace the old in a day or two of clear weather.

In wet seasons, petunias may become infested with aphids, which can be checked readily with malathion or nicotine sulphate. Wet weather or too much water may cause stem or root rot, especially in spring. Always avoid over watering your plants.

Free-flowering and readily grown from seed or from small, inexpensive seedlings, annuals return the most for your time, effort, and costs. And you can easily try out different kinds each year to fill your containers with fresh material.

Many annuals can be grown in containers, but keep in mind the matter of scale. Tall cosmos and African marigolds are out of place in window boxes, but not in large planters. Though most annuals are easy, some require special temperatures. Verbenas, dimorphothecas, nierem-bergias, portulacas, and California poppies like heat, while nemesias, stocks, pansies, and calceolarias do better when grown cool. In pot gardening, you can grow the cool-climate annuals for spring and early summer. In the warmest parts of the country, annuals can be treated as winter plants. Here are a few annuals well suited to containers.

Ageratum. Low annual, with fluffy lavender flowers, excellent for edging planters in sun or light shade. Avoid nitrogen; it encourages too much leaf growth.

Lobelia. Dwarf plant for edging, a favorite in window boxes. Small blue, lavender, or white flowers all season. Give sun or part shade and cut back after first floweringfor more bloom. Plants trail just enough for planting in hanging baskets with taller flowers in the center.

Cambridge Blue is a delightful sky-blue variety.

Marigolds. Tall African types and dwarf French hybrids in new and improved strains are excellent for window boxes and large planters. Give full sun and a lean soil for plentiful bloom. Yellow and orange dwarfs look well with blue ageratum, lobelias, or browallia.

Snapdragons. Hardy annuals, with dark green shiny leaves and spikes of red, maroon, yellow, orange, pink, rose, and white flowers. Pinch young plants to encourage branching, though this will delay flowering somewhat. They do well in part shade.

Stock. A fragrant annual with spikes of lavender, purple, pink, rose, and white flowers. Provide an alkaline, not too rich soil, to promote bloom. Arrange pots around living areas where the sweet scent can be enjoyed in the evenings.

Sweet Alyssum. An ideal edging plant for planters in white, lavender, purple, and pink. Plants bloom six weeks from seed. If tops are sheared after the first bloom, more flowers will appear. Royal carpet is a good purple, Little Gem, a white.

There are many other suitable annuals for pots, boxes, and planters-balsam, blue lace flower, blue salvia (aperennial where hardy), browallia, clarkia, cleome, di-morphotheca, feverfew, lantana (so treated), larkspur, linum or flax, love-in-a-mist, Madagascar periwinkle *(Vinca rosed),* nicotiana or flowering tobacco, nierem-bergia, patient Lucy, phlox, salpiglossis, scabiosa, schizan-thus, statice, venedium, verbena, and viscaria.

11. TREES, SHRUBS, AND VINES FOR ACCENT AND SCREENING

Trees, shrubs, and vines are basic plants for the container garden. They provide height and background, accent, and shade. Since nurserymen and garden centers offer them in bushel baskets, large tin cans or simply balled and burlapped, they are easily planted in permanent containers. Growing trees and shrubs in tubs and boxes is a widespread practice in climates with scant rainfall, like our Southwest and the Mediterranean countries, but gardeners everywhere can treat them as specimen plants. They lend distinction and grace to the large terrace or outdoor sitting area and are effective at doorways, along walks, on driveways, on terraces, and around swimming pools.

One great advantage of containers for trees and shrubs is that you can experiment with kinds that are tender in your climate. Oleanders, lemons, oranges, Chinese hibiscus, and camellias are all possibilities for northern gardeners. Unusual varieties of these and others can be tried, and you can give special attention to rare kinds.

Value of Trees

Trees contribute the element of height and the structural beauty of their trunks and lower branches, especially in winter, if they are deciduous. Some like stewartia and eucalyptus have colorful exfoliating barks that give winter interest. Trees also cast shade for sitting areas as well as for plants and create fascinating shadows on pavements and walls.

As a rule, small foliage or flowering trees-Japanese maples, crab-apples, Oriental cherries, and dogwoods-are best, since they require infrequent repotting. Slow growers, tupelo and ginkgo, are also valuable because they remain useful for long periods. Yet even large trees can be grown successfully in containers. Garden centers carry Norway and Crimson King maples, lindens, oaks, yellow-wood, plane trees, and honey-locusts. When the trees get too large, transplant them to the garden or give them away.

Value of Shrubs

Shrubs are easier to handle because they are smaller and require less space. For mass effects and backgrounds,

ILLUSTRATION XX

Simple wooden box holding a well-branched white pine tree. Covered with snow, it will take on added beauty. When too large for the box, it can be transferred to the open ground.

rely on large kinds, either hardy or tender, the latter for an exotic touch. Nowadays, shrubs, like trees, can be planted at any time because they are available in boxes, tins, or bushel baskets. This makes it easy to transfer them to tubs or boxes without disturbing the roots.

Allow for Evergreens

The container garden is not complete without some evergreens, especially in regions where the garden can be enjoyed on pleasant late autumn, winter, or early spring days. Well located evergreens are also appreciated from indoors. Balled and burlapped or container-grown, tree and shrub types can be obtained throughout the growing season. For interesting effects, combine evergreens with deciduous trees and shrubs-cherries, crab-apples, deut-zias, and viburnums. With careful clipping, hemlocks, pines, yews, and arborvitae can remain in the same containers for several years. Remember, too, to include some broad-leaved hollies, azaleas, rhododendrons, and camellias.

HARDY TREES

What trees are hardy in the colder regions of the North? Which are recommended for the warmer South? These general questions are difficult to answer because hardiness is variable; each section of the country has its own definition. As gardeners, we are constantly learning what will and will not do in the areas in which we live. Nevertheless, there are certain trees that are considered hardy in regions where temperatures go well below freezing. For these sections, here are some of the more desirable kinds:

Birches. Graceful trees for containers. Clumps of the native gray, white or paper, or weeping European birches are desirable for the contrasting bark. Small leaves cast light shade.

Crab-apples. Lovely hardy flowering trees, with red, pink, purple, or white blossoms in spring and colorful fruits in fall, much favored by birds. The smallest one, which can be pruned to picturesque form, is the white-flowering Sargent crab-apple, as broad as it is tall. Choice hybrids include Dorothea, Dolgo, Flame, Hopa, and Katherine.

Dogwoods. Many kinds, including flowering dogwood, with white or pink flowers in spring, brilliant fall coloring, and interesting winter form. The Japanese kousa dogwood blooms later and continues for several weeks. For the West Coast, there is the upright Pacific dogwood. Cornelian cherry, a true dogwood, bears tiny yellow flowers in early spring.

Dove Tree or Davidia. Where reliably hardy (a specimen at Arnold Arboretum, Boston, blooms periodically), an unusual tree, with large white bracts among heart-shaped leaves in spring. Requires special care, but is worth the effort.

Franklinia or Gordonia. Like the dove tree, also requiring special attention. Single, camellia-like, cream-white flowers open in late summer and continue until frost. Leaves are colorful in fall. Barely surviving winters around Boston, this is reliably hardy from New York City southward.

Fringe Tree. Large shrub or small tree, with fluffy, white flowers appearing with unfolding foliage in late spring. Shows up strikingly against evergreens.

Ginkgo. One of the best, very hardy and slow growing with a fascinating form. Also called maidenhair tree, it transplants easily. A fastigiate variation, the Sentry Gingko, will give accent.

Golden-Chain Tree or Laburnum. Small ornamental tree with pendulous, wisteria-like, golden flowers in spring. It will attract much attention in a large plant box.

Golden-Rain Tree or Koelreuteria. One of few yellow-flowering trees for the North. Compound leaves are highlighted by upright panicles in midsummer, followed bypods that change through several colors. Golden-rain withstands drought.

Hawthorns. Many kinds, with showy red, pink, or white flowers in spring. Outstanding is the English hawthorn, including the red Paul's Scarlet and Arnold hawthorn with white flower clusters. Washington thorn has bright red berries in fall.

Hollies. Pyramidal broad-leaved evergreens with handsome foliage and sparkling red berries. American holly is hardier than English, but both have forms with variegated leaves and yellow or orange berries. All withstand formal clipping.

Japanese Red Maple. Dainty, with divided dark leaves and a horizontal habit. Varieties have deep-cut green leaves *(Acer palmatum dissectum)* or purple foliage *(A. p. atropurpureum).* Much grown in containers on the West Coast.

Japanese Snowbell or Styrax. Small and spreading, with myriads of exquisite white bells in early summer hanging from underneath the horizontal branches.

Japanese Tree Lilac. The last of the lilacs to bloom, with large, fragrant, cream-white tresses in early summer. Very hardy and slow growing, it can be trained with one or several trunks.

Magnolias. Many kinds with showy flowers. Earliest to bloom is the star magnolia in white or pink. If spring frost threatens, move to shelter during night. Next to flower is the common saucer magnolia in white, pink, rose, or purple. This has an interesting habit and soft gray bark. Sweet bay magnolia produces fragrant, cream-white flowers over a period of weeks during the summer. Attractive dark green leaves are whitish beneath.

Moraine Locust. Recently introduced variety, with fine compound leaves and an open, graceful habit. Fast growing, and pest-free with neither thorns nor messy seed pods. Sunburst locust, another variety, is noted for its golden-yellow tips.

Mountain Ash. Showiest is the European with a loose habit and white flowers in spring followed by rich clusters of orange-red fruits. Fast-growing plants offer filtered shade.

Oriental Flowering Cherries. Small trees, with single or double, pink, rose, or white flowers in spring. Unique is the weeping cherry, with very early pink blossoms. Variety Kwanzan, a narrow, upright grower, has large double blooms resembling roses.

Pines. Choice depends on climate and personal preference. The red, pitch, Scotch, Austrian, and Japanese black pines are seashore subjects, but all pines take well to container culture if kept moist and not neglected in winter. They do best in sun and can be pruned or sheared.

Poplars. Fast-growing, weak-wooded trees, easily replaced because they are readily obtainable at reasonable prices. The slender Lombardy poplar can be planted for accent or a hedge. All easy for the container garden.

Redbud or Judas Tree. Small, with rose-pink flowers in tight clusters and heart-shaped leaves. The eastern common redbud is the hardiest, but in milder climates the Chinese redbud is equally lovely.

Russian Olive. Admired for silvery leaves and the crooked trunk and branches it develops. Very hardy and vigorous, fine for the seashore because it withstands wind and salt spray.

Silverbell or Halesia. Upright tree with tiny bells in white or pink at dogwood and tulip time. Locate where it can be observed closely.

Scholar Tree or Sophora. A member of the pea family, with compound leaves and cream-white flowers in midsummer. Tolerates dust and soot of cities.

Sourwood or Oxydendrum. Small summer-flowering tree, with drooping clusters of small, fragrant flowers and lustrous leaves that turn scarlet in autumn. In containers, specimens can easily be provided with the acid soil they need.

Stewartias. In summer, the Japanese stewartia has white

Window box with nasturtiums and flowering cactus at Horv,
Switzerland

Lemon trees in large decorative pots at
the Florentine villa of Mr. and Mrs.
Timothy Mather Spelman

Boxes of red geraniums on the histi Chapel Bridge in Lucerne, Switzerl;

Geraniums in huge concrete containers in the heart of Stockholm

Raised boxes and tubs with geraniums, petunias, and English ivy at the Ballinger Gallery in Rock-port, Massachusetts *(Top)*. Pink hydrangeas in earthenware jugs in a small Florentine garden *(Left)*. Vivid scarlet geraniums in boxes on the terrace of Mrs., Christine Connell *(Bottom)*

A shrine to the Madonna with tuberous begonias in clay pots in the garden of Miss Mary A. Sullivan

urtium plants in plastic pots above the ray of the Au Beauchamp
Restaurant in n *(Top left)*

Otaheite orange in a jardinière on the top terrace of Mr. and Mrs.
Joel E. Har-*Top right)*

ted strawberry jar with strawberry plants s home o£ Mr. and Mrs. C. A. B. Hal-*n (Bottom)*

Hanging basket of browallia

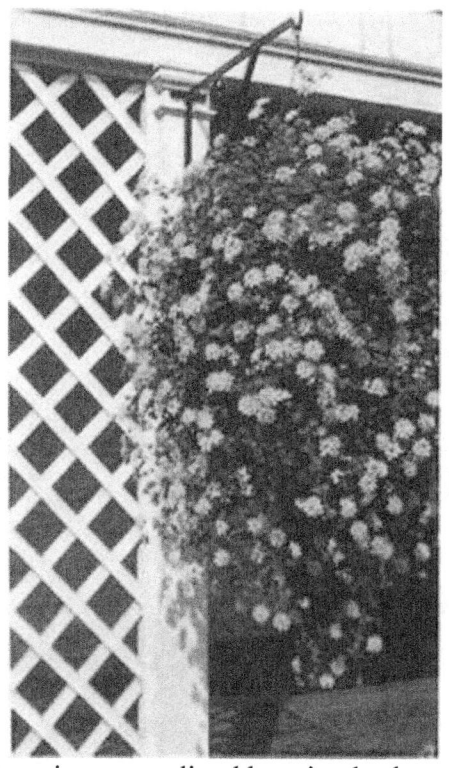

Lush purple lantana in a moss-lined hanging basket on the porch of Mrs. Eleanor M. Buttars

Window and plant boxes of vivid red petunias

Window boxes of pink geraniums with dark red coleus and white sweet alyssum at the Commodore Restaurant *(Top left)*

Yellow-leaved coleus with geranium Mine. Languth and purple sweet alyssum *(Top right)*

Pink geraniums, lobelias, and sweet alyssum at the Commodore Restaurant in Beverly, Massachusetts *(Bottom left)*

Red geraniums and white petunias in a box *(Bottom right)*

blooms with orange stamens, and the showy stewartia has white blossoms with purple stamens. Both have colorful autumn foliage and rough barks.

Weeping Willows. Among the best trees for rooftops because they withstand wind. Fast growing, they need periodic replacement, but young plants are moderately priced. The Golden Weeping Willow has bright yellow twigs in winter and chartreuse catkins in early spring.

This is only a partial list of hardy trees for the container garden. Almost any kind can be grown if in scale and given the necessary care. Do not overlook fastigiate forms-upright lindens, oaks, sugar and Norway maples -since these take up little space.

TENDER TREES

Tender trees are commonly grown in warmer regions, where they remain outdoors all year. In colder areas, as container subjects, they require shelter in winter. As a group, they are popular with both southern and northern gardeners.

Acacias. Many kinds of acacias are treasured for their feathery yellow flowers in winter and early spring. Fast growing, they require a cool greenhouse or plant room in the North in winter.

Bullbay Magnolia. A highly ornamental evergreen magolia, much grown in the South, with large dark green leaves and huge fragrant white flowers. Where not hardy, a most worthwhile container plant.

California Pepper Tree. A semi pendulous small tree, with fernlike, olive-green leaves and hanging clusters of long-lasting, rose-colored berries. A native of Peru, it withstands heat and dryness, even poor soil, as well as severe pruning. Much planted as a street tree in southern Europe.

Citrus. Glossy-leaved trees, with small, scented flowers and decorative, lasting fruits. Orange, lemon, kumquat, tangerine, lime, and others do well in tubs and boxes. The dwarf Otaheite or Tahiti orange and the Ponderosa lemon are small types.

Crape Myrtle. The "lilac of the South," a shrub or small tree, with great tresses of crinkled blooms in pink, red, purple, and white all summer long. Container-grown in the North, it must be wintered in a cool frost-free place. It withstands severe pruning.

Eucalyptus. Rapid-growing, drought-resistant trees with leathery aromatic leaves and peeling bark. Replacements of container specimens are easily made.

Fig. The edible fig of southern Europe is fine for containers in the North. Large, coarse leaves are light green; the bark is a pleasing gray. *Japanese Privet.* A handsome tall shrub or small tree, with glossy, dark green leaves and panicles of white flowers, followed by black berries. It is often confused with the less handsome glossy privet *(Ligustrum lucidum).*

Loquat. A Japanese tree with long, leathery, strong-veined leaves and tasty orange-yellow fruits. An excellent tub specimen for terraces or patios, as often seen in southern Europe.

Norfolk Island Pine. A pyramidal, horizontal evergreen with sharp-pointed leaves. Much grown as a pot or tub plant in greenhouses in the North.

Olive. Picturesque tree with twisted, gnarled trunk and branches as it gets older. Leaves are small, thick and evergreen, olive-green above and silvery below. Slow-growing plants bear black fruits that fall when ripe.

Pacific Madrone {Arbutus menziesi). An attractive broad-leaved evergreen, with fragrant, heathlike, white flowers in six-inch panicles surmounting large, glossy leaves. Chocolate-brown bark sheds like that of the plane tree. Difficult to move, plants are best transplanted as seedlings under eighteen inches.

Palms. Often seen in the North in public parks and botanical gardens in tubs. Graceful with slender trunks, often curving, and arching leaves. Some are small, as thelady palm *(Raphis excelsa)* which attains six to ten feet. All grow easily and withstand neglect.

Sweet Bay or Grecian Laurel. The true laurel of the ancient Greeks, familiar as a clipped tubbed specimen, often with a single trunk and pungent, dark green leaves. Tough and easy-to-grow, appropriate for formal doorways, hotels, or public buildings. Requires a cool place in winter in the North.

Rubber Plant. A familiar house plant in the North with large glossy leaves. Include some variegated forms for color highlights.

HARDY SHRUBS

With trees, shrubs are needed for background, mass effects, and shade. Every container garden also requires some hardy needle and broadleaved evergreens for year-round color. In summer in the North, these can be supplemented with camellias, pittosporums, podocarpus, oleanders, sweet bays, and citrus plants. Include deciduous types for bloom and the interest of the branches in winter. Here is a recommended but far from complete list of possibilities.

Arborvitae. Versatile evergreen for the portable garden. Inexpensive, hardy, and quick-growing, it is ideal for hedges or background or for closing off sections. Little Gem, a variety of American arborvitae, is low and compact, a foot high, but spreading several feet.

Azaleas. Brilliant flowering shrubs requiring an acid soil. They also make good container plants in alkaline areas since soil can be prepared for them. Plants take shade, but flower better in sun. Always keep moist, since fibrous roots resent drying out.

Brooms or Cytisus. Green arching stems, with abundant flowers in spring. Require full sun and a light, sandy soil. Both the showy Warminster broom, with yellow flowers, and the familiar golden Scotch broom are dependable.

Cotoneasters. Interesting with a world of possibilities. Flowers are inconspicuous but glossy leaves and colorful berries are attractive. Rock spray cotoneaster has flat, horizontally arching branches. The small-leaved evergreen cotoneaster can be arranged around trees in planters and large boxes to avoid bareness.

Enkianthus. Handsome with small, bell-shaped flowers in pendulous clusters, fine to see close at hand. Lustrous leaves become fiery red in autumn. An acid-soil plant, requiring the same culture as azaleas.

Fothergillas or Bottlebrushes. Small shrubs with white flowers in spring and large, coarse leaves that color in autumn. Dwarf fothergilla *(Fothergilla gardeni)* attains three feet, but the large fothergilla *(F. major)* grows taller.

Hollies. Handsome plants, with shiny foliage and bright berries. Japanese holly *(Ilex crenata)* has dark green leaves; the convex-leaved Japanese holly has small, rounded, highly polished leaves; Haller's Japanese holly is a small, compact variety; and Kingsville is a true dwarf. Inkberry, another shrub holly, has lustrous evergreen leaves, an open habit, and black berries in fall. Leaves turn bronzy-purple in winter.

Japanese Flowering Quinces. Many varieties, including dwarfs with vermilion, scarlet, pink, rose, red, apricot, and white blossoms. These easy shrubs are primarily desired for early spring vivid color.

Japanese Yews. Among the best evergreens for hardiness, ease of culture and tolerance of sun or shade. There are upright, columnar, spreading, and low forms; all have dark green needles and are excellent for contrast with flowers. These are hardy in the North, but be sure to water all container plants in winter when soil is not frozen. The upright, rounded Hatfield and the columnar Hicks yews make good hedges. Where hardy, English yews can be substituted.

Pieris. The upright Japanese has hanging white flower clusters and bronzy-red new spring growth. The mountain pieris is lower and rounded, with upright white flower heads. Both have attractive foliage and are dependable the year-round.

Roses. Many kinds are suited to containers. Floribun-das are more floriferous than hybrid teas and can be used as low hedges or in groups. On terraces and patios include hybrid teas for color, form, and fragrance if you can face the spraying, etc. Where hardiness is questionable, store in a cool place, as a garage or closed-in breezeway, in winter. In pots and window boxes grow the delightful miniatures.

Rhododendrons. Broad, glossy, evergreen leaves and showy flowers in red, rose, pink, purple, or white. Give sun for a few hours a day for richer bloom. In winter, put in a protected spot to avoid windburning. Rhododendrons need a peaty, humusy, acid soil and plenty of water.

Spice Bush. Moisture-loving, with small, yellow, pungent flower clusters in early spring. The leaves unfolding later are large, neat, and aromatic.

Summer Sweet or Clethra. Intensely fragrant, white or pink spikes appear for several weeks in summer. Give an acid soil and plenty of water.

Viburnums. A dependable group with attractive leaves, white flower clusters (some fragrant as *V. carlesi and carl-cephalum),* and colorful berries. The large double file viburnum has flat flower heads along horizontal branches. The Japanese snowball is a showy double form.

TENDER SHRUBS

Tender shrubs-camellias, gardenias, lemons, and oleanders-are important in the container garden. Here are just a few of the many possibilities.

Camellias. Outstanding evergreen shrubs for containers. Acid-loving, they need winter protection in the North. Where hardy, tubbed plants provide accent at doorways and on terraces. Waxy blooms in various colors appear from fall through spring against shiny, dark green leaves.

Chinese Hibiscus. Colorful favorites in Florida, Southern California, and Hawaii, with shiny, heart-shaped, coarse leaves and dramatic hollyhock-like flowers in pink and rose, white, peach, orange, and yellow, single and double. Plants can take hard pruning.

Citrus. Many shrubby kinds, all good for containers, they can be trained as trees or shrubs. In Europe, oranges and lemons are ornamental features of estate and palace gardens. Small kinds are charming in pots.

Hollies. Several tender kinds, like the evergreen Chinese, Dahoon, and Yunnan hollies, are attractive for both leaves and fruits.

Holly Osmanthus. A choice evergreen with lustrousleaves and scented yellow-green flowers. Good for small, neatly clipped hedges. Consider the variegated form and the variety, Fortune's Osmanthus, with larger leaves to four inches. Indispensable for containers in the South and the West Coast.

Hydrangeas. Fine for tubs, these plants have huge, showy, long-lasting flowers in pink, blue, lavender, and white. Plants are deciduous and require cool storage in winter, though they take temperatures to zero without bud killing if cold spells are short. They need rich, hu-musy soil, abundant moisture, and are recommended for shade. The blues have an especially cool appeal on hot, summer days.

Japanese Aucuba. Evergreen, popular for pots and planters in Europe, especially in front of cafes in Paris. A delightful variegated form is the Gold-Dust Tree. It is best in shade or part shade, for leaves turn yellow in full sun. Red berries appear in fall.

Nandina. Oriental shrub, with fine-cut leaves and clusters of red berries, sometimes called Chinese sacred bamboo. Berries last long after the delicate, compound leaves fall.

Oleander. A traditional evergreen tub plant with long, narrow, shiny leaves and single or double fragrant flowers. Requires a frost proof, well lighted place in the North inwinter. Oleanders can be trained as standards, as they are often seen on streets in Greece.

Rosemary. Mediterranean shrub with narrow, aromatic leaves that are dark green above and gray-white below. Thrives in sun and slightly dry soil; becomes leggy in shade in rich soil. Plants develop a natural asymmetrical habit, but may be clipped. The variety, Heavenly Blue, has semi trailing branches and small flowers, deeper blue than the species.

Ruscus. Called also butcher's broom, a low-growing evergreen that is a common pot plant in patios of Mediterranean countries. Stiff habit and leathery, prickly, pointed leaves. Rugged plants withstand hot sun, shade, poor soil, and drought.

VINES FOR SCREENING

Vines and climbers perform significant roles in container gardens. They cover walls, fences, and other vertical spaces. Attractive in flower and foliage, they also form interesting patterns, cover unsightly areas, cut off undesirable views, provide screening for privacy, and create shade for plants.

There are hardy and tender vines, depending on where you live. Stephanotis, clerodendron, wax plant, allamanda, poet's jasmine, and bougainvillea are tender in the North. Hardy vines include English ivy, Virginia creeper, Boston ivy, climbing euonymus and Dutchman's pipe, which are grown for their foliage. For quick one-season effects, there are annual climbers-morning-glories, moon vines, cardinal climber, scarlet runner beans, climbing nasturtiums, cobaeas, and sweet peas.

Wisteria. A most spectacular hardy vine, with long, pendulous clusters in spring in purple, lavender, pink, and white. The Chinese wisteria, which flowers without leaves, is less hardy than the Japanese, which blooms with foliage. Vigorous plants require large containers and constant pruning to encourage bloom and also keep them in hand. Tree wisteria is most decorative when grown in a tub.

Hybrid Clematis. Handsome hardy vines, with large, starlike blooms, in lavender, purple, red, pink, or white in late spring and through the summer. Nurserymen offer hybrids in pots, easy to transfer to larger containers. Provide a well-drained soil with lime added.

Star or Confederate Jasmine. A pot plant in the North, though hardy in the South, with small, star-shaped, pin-wheeled, fragrant flowers that smother the glossy evergreen leaves. Give a large pot or tub and place where the scented flowers can be enjoyed close at hand. Thrives in sun or shade.

Stephanotis. Glossy-leaved, with scented, white, waxy flowers. Not hardy in the North, keep in a cool place in winter and water sparingly.

A llamanda. A tropical vine, with shiny leaves and large, tubular, yellow flowers produced freely all year around. In the North, tender plants require a greenhouse. Vines like sun and rich soil, but are not otherwise difficult.

Bougainvillea. Also called Chinese paper flower, with vibrant, fiery flowers in magenta, purple, rose, pink, red, and white. Not particular as to soil, but needs sun and plenty of water when growing. Rest in cool place in winter by keeping on dry side.

Gloriosa. A tuberous-rooted tender vine, with red and yellow lily-like flowers. Hardy in the South, plants are treated as pot subjects only in the North. For this, start tubers in large pots in March or April and bring to a sunny spot outdoors when freezing weather has passed. Provide trellis support, water regularly, and feed with liquid fertilizer when plants are half grown. Store bulbs in their own pots in a frost proof place and start them again the following spring.

Passion Vine. Odd and beautiful flowers on quick-growing plants that need rich soil and large containers. In the North, this is often treated as an annual, but plants may be kept in a cool room during winter, where they will continue to bloom. The fragrant flowers close at night, but will remain open if melted wax is dripped on the inside. After treatment, flowers make fine corsages or can be floated in bowls of water.

12. PERENNIALS, HERBS, AND VEGETABLES FOR CONTAINERS

Herbaceous perennials are valuable in the container garden. In planters, raised beds, and large boxes, they contribute greatly to the garden design with their distinctive foliage and attractive flowers. As a group, perennials are adapted to a variety of conditions, tolerating sun or shade, moist or dry locations. For the most part, they are hardy, but some require winter covering.

Select some perennials with good all-season foliage. When daylilies, peonies, phlox, coral-bells, gas plant, astilbe, and hardy candytuft finish flowering, their leaves remain attractive. With Oriental poppies, bleeding hearts and primroses, the leaves turn yellow once blooming is over, though this does not mean they are undesirable. Bare spots left by them can be concealed by other plants like quick-growing annuals.

Perennials like daylilies and iris thrive where it is hot; lupines, delphiniums, and astilbes prefer cooler temperatures. You can have some biennials, too-foxgloves, canterbury-bells, sweet williams and verbascums-and discard them after flowering.

Today, nurserymen and garden centers offer mature perennial and biennial plants in tins, baskets, tar paper, papier-mache, and other temporary containers. They provide for quick, colorful effects.

PERENNIALS

Acanthus or Bear's Breech. Tall and striking from southern Europe, whose leaf the ancient Greeks adapted for the capitals of Corinthian columns. Arching, deep-cut, thistlelike leaves, two feet long, shining dark green, are surmounted with tall, white, rose-tinged spikes. Give plants large pots with good drainage and full sun. Not hardy in the North where they need winter protection.

Asters. Handsome with starry blossoms for rich purple, lavender, rose, pink, and white autumn displays. Many varieties vary from nine inches to four or more feet. Plants need full sun and respond to feeding and watering, but are otherwise easy. They are best divided each spring.

Bearded Iris. Number one favorite, beloved for its exquisite blooms in rainbow colors. Hardy and easy to grow, spearlike leaves provide accent among other plants. Clumps need dividing every third year. Borers can be

ILLUSTRATION XXI
Roses in large green tubs on the terrace of Mr. and Mrs. Arno H.
Nehling. Tubs are on wheels so they can be moved about.

controlled with repeated DDT sprayings, starting in early spring.

Chrysanthemums. Free-flowering and invaluable for the pot garden. With these alone, you can enjoy riotous color from August even to December. Grow your own or buy plants in bud from commercial growers. They move easily when in bloom, if you take care to keep them moist. After flowering, plant in garden or cold frame and give winter protection or discard the roots like annuals.

Daylilies or Hemerocallis. Thriving in hot and cold climates, in shade or full sun. Straplike foliage remains attractive all season. For warmer regions there are evergreen varieties. Trumpet flowers, mostly yellow and crimson, open over a long period, even though each bloom stays fresh but one day. The Greek name, hemerocallis, means "beautiful for a day."

Delphinium. Regal plant with tall, stately spikes in shades of blue, purple, and white. Sow seed in February or March for flowering plants the same season or purchase seedlings in spring for large containers. Seed sown in June or July will bloom the following summer. Delphiniums need sun and staking up to their heads. Try some of the gorgeous Pacific Hybrids.

Hostas. These handsome perennials have broad leaves, green or variegated. Low growing types are ideal to edgelarge planters. Hardy, pest free and easy. Consider the August lily, with fragrant white bells in summer; Honey-bells, with tall spikes of purple flowers; and Thomas Hogg, with green leaves edged white.

Phlox. Dependable for bright color in July, August, and September. Thrives in sun or partial shade and needs plenty of water. Allowed to dry out, phlox wilts and the lower leaves turn brown. Comes in pink, salmon, rose, red, scarlet, lavender, purple, and white. If tips are pinched when plants are six to nine inches high, flower heads will be more numerous, though smaller.

Rose Mallow or Hibiscus. Spectacular for tall, bold effects. Large flowers, like single hollyhocks, appear during late summer and fall in red, rose, pink, and white. Hybrids measure nine and more inches across. Good for screening hedges. Plants like rich soil, abundant moisture, and full sun though partial shade is endured.

BIENNIALS

Canterbury-Bells. Choice biennial, with long-lasting bells in purple, lavender, blue, pink, and white. Worth the effort, even if they die after flowering. In the spring, garden centers offer budded specimens. For dramatic compositions, group several together. You can grow your own from seed sown in June or July.

ILLUSTRATION XXII
Chrysanthemums in painted wooden tubs at the inviting gate of Mr.
and Mrs. Arno H. Nehrling.

Foxgloves. Delightful, with tall spikes covered with bells. Sow seed in June or July and winter young plants in cold frame or garden, covering with marsh hay or evergreen branches. Old-fashioned kinds have bells on one side of the spikes, but the new English hybrids have flowers all around the stems. Pot-grown rosettes are available in spring.

Other perennials and biennials to grow are heuchera or coral-bells, veronica, showy stonecrop or sedum, helen-ium, Japanese iris, scabiosa, shasta daisy, lythrum, platy-codon or balloon flower, pentstemon, peony, Oriental poppy, monarda or bee-balm, lavender, liatris, tritoma, heliopsis, anthemis, gaillardia, gas plant, columbine, and butterfly weed. Do not overlook such rock garden plants as arabis, aubretia, basket-of-gold, snow-in-the-summer, thyme, viola, ajuga, dianthus, primrose, and auricula. (A well-illustrated catalog will help you select.)

HERBS FOR FRAGRANCE

If you like herbs and enjoy them in cooking, you can have an herb garden in containers. Try sun-loving rosemary, marjoram, parsley, sage, fennel, mint and chives in individual pots or tubs or with other plants in large boxes. Grow with them some of the scented-leaved geraniums, like rose, cinnamon, nutmeg, lemon, apple, and peppermint.

A few years ago, Mrs. Frances R. Williams of Winchester, Massachusetts, who was unable to raise herbs in her shady garden, decided to try them on her nine-foot square porch, which had sun until late afternoon. She used twelve low bushel baskets and four egg cases, each filled with half-rotted compost to within four inches of the top. Then three inches of fertilized soil was spread on top.

In two of the egg cases, Mrs. Williams planted summer savory, and a dozen basil plants in the other two. Dill, lettuce-leaved basil, narrow-leaved French thyme, and sweet marjoram were also grown. All yielded enough for summer salads and winter drying. In a few of the other baskets, Mrs. Williams planted small-fruited red cherry, red and yellow pear, and yellow plum varieties of tomatoes. Since the deep containers held moisture for a long time, they did not require daily watering. On the shady side of the house, bushel baskets, filled mostly with compost, were planted with open heads of leaf and Bibb lettuce.

VEGETABLES

Vegetables can also be grown in containers, if only for novel effect. Purple kale and cabbage are attractive and always arouse curiosity. Grouped around a small pool or on a table, white-fruiting eggplants in individual pots are charming. Rhubarb in large planters or boxes will make a bold accent for the contemporary terrace. In containers, the feathery leaves of carrots, the linear foliage of onions, and the fruits of tomatoes, especially the small kinds, are fun to look at and eat.

The pot garden offers an excellent opportunity to grow miniature plants, a new form of gardening that is increasing in popularity. In England, where growing miniatures has become a hobby, it appeals strongly to older people, who like to fuss with tiny plants in old stone sinks and other containers raised to waist level.

CACTI AND WATERLILIES

In hot climates with little rainfall, cacti and succulents can be the answer. They can be grown, too, in other areas, particularly by gardeners who like to travel without worrying about the container plants they leave behind. Foliage patterns and forms of these plants are fascinating, and many extraordinary compositions can be achieved. Easy to grow, they need a lean soil and are best in small pots.

Water lilies and other water plants can be grown in small low tubs, perhaps one water lily with a specimen of Cyprus or floating hyacinth. In a large tub, Egyptian lotus, with its enormous leaves and blooms rising several feet above the surface of the water, is a handsome sight.

BONSAI

Bonsai or Japanese dwarf trees are also container plants, but these comprise a specialty that is a study and art in itself. It is, however, increasingly popular, and books are available that tell how to train and maintain these dwarf trees and shrubs. Plants can be purchased from nurserymen who specialize in this unusual aspect of container gardening.

13. BULBS FOR BEAUTIFUL POT PLANTS

As a group, bulbs are outstanding plants-colorful, showy, and generally easy to grow. Many have evergreen foliage; with others, the leaves ripen after flowering and the bulbs are stored and started again, year after year. Some bulbs are hardy, others, tender, though what is and is not hardy in a particular area is a matter of winter temperature averages. In cold regions, tender types-tuberous begonias, gloxinias, calla lilies, and gloriosa lilies - can be treated like summer container plants. This gives the gardener a wide variety to grow from earliest spring to late fall.

Dutch Bulbs

Included in this group are crocus, snowdrops, eranthis or winter aconites, chionodoxas, scillas, grape hyacinths, leucojums or snowflakes, Dutch hyacinths, daffodils, and tulips, the pride of northern spring gardens. Though hardy, they are not adapted to containers outdoors where temperatures drop much below freezing. They require the protection of a shed, unheated cellar or cold frame. Pots can also be dug into a trench in the ground for the winter and covered with a thick blanket of marsh hay or straw. Where temperatures do not go below freezing, Dutch bulbs can be left outdoors in containers over the winter.

For best results, start with fresh, firm, large-sized bulbs each fall. Insure good drainage in the bottom of each pot and use a light soil with bone meal added. If in clay pots, plunge during the rooting period in damp peat moss to prevent rapid drying out. If this occurs too often, roots will be injured and flowers will be poor. When weather permits, after the danger of freezing passes, put containers outside where they are to flower or in a nursery row until they reach the bud stage. After blooming, place containers where foliage can ripen unseen.

For fragrance, concentrate on Dutch hyacinths, excellent for bedding large planter boxes or raised beds. Daffodils look well grouped around trees or large shrubs, as birches and forsythias. Tulips, formal in character, combine delightfully with pansies, violas, wall flowers, forget-me-nots, marguerites, English daisies, and annual candytuft.

As already indicated, in cold areas, Dutch bulbs cannot

ILLUSTRATION XXIII *(above left)*

Geraniums in an old-fashioned black kettle, an example of effective treatment of just one container plant.
ILLUSTRATION XXIV *(center)*
Luxuriant tuberous begonias in an antique brass kettle on the shady porch of Mr. and Mrs. William Davis.
ILLUSTRATION XXV *(below right)*
Decorative basket placed around a clay pot containing fuchsia Mme. Cornelissen. This red-and-white variety is one of the best for sun.

be potted or planted in small window boxes and left outdoors unprotected for the winter. They can, however, be set out in large planters and boxes, deep and wide enough to contain plenty of soil. Containers should be one and a half to two feet deep and about two feet wide. Set bulbs, with at least six inches of soil above them, planting them early enough in the fall so that they can make root growth before soil freezes hard. In penthouse gardens in New York City, Dutch bulbs have been grown successfully in this way, but it is always a risk. It makes no difference whether containers are made of wood, concrete, or other material; it is the amount of soil they hold that counts.

Actually, it is not the freezing of the soil that injures bulbs (this occurs in open ground), but it is the pressure and counter pressure exerted by frost on the sides of containers, which are firm and do not give. As a result, bulbs are bruised and thrust out of the soil, their roots torn. Where there is no hard freeze, but sufficient cold weather, hardy bulbs can be grown successfully in containers of small size.

Achimenes. Warmth-loving trailing plants with neat leaves and tubular flowers in blue, lavender, red and white. Related to gloxinias and African violets, they are nice in hanging baskets and window boxes or in pots on tables, shelves, or wall brackets. Start the small tubers in-142 doors and give plants a sheltered spot with protection from strong sun and wind. Achimenes, an old standby in the South, is worthy of more frequent planting.

Agapanthus or Blue Lily of the Nile. Fleshy-rooted evergreen plant, with strap leaves, often grown in tubs and urns on terraces and steps during the summer, when the tall blue spikes unfold. Culture is easy, but plants require a well-lighted, frost proof room or greenhouse in winter. This is an old-time favorite, often seen in gardens of Europe.

BULBS FOR BEAUTIFUL POT PLANTS

Calla Lily. Showy, hardy outdoors in warmer regions, but a tender pot plant in the North. Most familiar is the white one with large, shiny, heart-shaped leaves. Start bulbs indoors in February or March in rich soil and, when weather settles, transfer to large pots and take outdoors. Calla lilies do well in full sun or part shade, are heavy feeders and need much water. There is also a dainty yellow with white-spotted leaves. Rest bulbs after foliage ripens and grow again.

Dahlias. Colorful and free-flowering, they provide bounteous cut blooms. Tall, large-flowering kinds can be grown only in large planters and boxes, but the dwarfs, even freer flowering, are excellent in small containers.

Attaining one to two feet tall, they grow easily from tubers in average soil in sun or part shade. They may also be raised from seed sown indoors in February. If tubers are stored in peat or sand in a cool, frost proof place, they can be grown for years. Check bulbs during winter, and if shriveling, sprinkle lightly.

Gladiolus. Summer-flowering with spear like leaves and many hued spikes. Corms can be planted in containers outdoors after danger of frost is passed. Set them six inches apart and four to six inches deep. If several containers are planted every two to three weeks, there will be a succession of bloom. Stake stems before flowers open. After the leaves turn brown, or there is a frost, lift corms, cut off foliage and dust with DDT to control thrips. Store corms in a dry place at 45 to 55 degrees F.

Gloxinias. Summer-flowering and tender with large, tubular blooms of red, pink, lavender, purple, or white, and broad velvety rosettes of leaves. Start tubers indoors and don't take outside until weather is warm. Since the leaves are easily broken or injured by wind or rain, put plants in a sheltered spot. The low broad eaves of contemporary houses, with restricted sun, offer an appropriate setting for rows of pots or window boxes filled with gay gloxinias.

Lilies. Gorgeous and hardy, with blooms in many colors. It is now possible to have a lily container garden, with flowers from May to frost. Open the season with the dainty *Lilium pumilum* and continue with madonnas, Golden Chalice hybrids, Olympic hybrids, auratums, and specios-ums. Lilies can be planted in fall, like daffodils and tulips, and they will also flower from bulbs set out in early spring. In cold regions, the rules for Dutch bulbs outdoors in winter apply also to lilies, which do well in large planters, two feet wide and two feet deep. Group several of one variety for a good effect. Plant smaller sizes in individual six or eight inch pots to be wintered in cold frames. Plant larger sizes in eight or ten inch pots. After flowering put containers out of sight while stalks ripen.

Nurserymen and florists offer pot-grown lilies in early spring ready to plant in containers without disturbance of roots. Try combining several in large containers, with English ivy, vinca, grape ivy, dwarf annuals, or other low plants for softening effects. After flowering, bulbs can be planted in the garden, grown again in containers or given to friends.

Tuberose. Tender and summer-flowering with narrow foliage and tall spikes of single or double white flowers, fragrant and long-lasting. Where seasons are short, bulbs are best started indoors six to eight weeks before plantingoutdoors. Plant in six-inch pots and feed with liquid fertilizer. Tuberoses need a rich, well-drained soil and full sun and staking of the tall spike. Since bulbs do not flower well a second year start with fresh stock each spring.

14. THE CHARM OF WINDOW BOXES

Visitors to Europe, flower-minded or not, return with enthusiasm for the gay window boxes they have seen-the red geraniums in Germany and Austria, the tuberous begonias of Switzerland, these so perfect they seem to have been moved right out of a catalog! In fact, Switzerland suggests glorious possibilities for this country. How beautiful our cities might be if railroad terminals, apartment houses, department stores, and office buildings could all be decorated with window boxes, as they are in that small mountain country.

With centuries of tradition behind them, Europeans have had rich experience in growing plants in boxes. We see them high above the streets of London, Dublin, Copenhagen, Paris, Rome, Vienna, Heidelberg, and Geneva. Along narrow, winding streets, they are a charming decoration throughout the growing season. In spring, daffodils, tulips, hyacinths, pansies, wall flowers, and English

ILLUSTRATION XXVI
Dow boxes with all geraniums and petunias at the home of J.
Henry L. Giles

daisies appear in profusion; in summer, geraniums everywhere radiate their dependable brilliance.

Those who live in farmhouses share the enthusiasm. In Germany, Austria, and Switzerland, potted geraniums, grown indoors in winter, are moved out to window boxes in summer, but still kept in pots. Sometimes boxes are solid structures, more often, they are of latticework painted green or white. With cool weather, potted plants are put back on window sills, where they remain-and flower-until spring.

In enchanting medieval Dinkelsbuhl in southern Germany, I recall a green high-gabled house with boxes of geraniums and tuberous begonias at windows on four floors, including the single one below the steep peak. In that village, even tiny windows are adorned with potted geraniums.

Gardens in Window Boxes

In this country, boxes at windows offer apartment dwellers the enjoyment of a little garden from within or without. If you live in just one room or on a very small property, you, too, can have a window-box garden filled in spring with pansies and primroses, in summer with petunias or fuchsias, and in fall with chrysanthemums. In winter, greens and berries, like bittersweet or Californiapepper berries with pine, give color. Where English ivy is not exposed to wind, it can provide trailing green all winter.

Size and Materials

To be serviceable, a window box must be large enough to accommodate comfortably the plants of your choice. Small shallow boxes are not worthwhile, because they hold too little soil and so dry out quickly. In hot summer sun, a small amount of soil also tends to overheat.

For good results, a window box ought to be at least three to four feet long but not more than six feet. Ii larger, it is too heavy to suspend and secure properly, and it cannot be lifted easily, even by two people. Boxes resting on broad window ledges and on firm porch railings might be eight feet long, but hardly more since moving them becomes too hazardous. Keep to a minimum depth of eight to nine inches, with a width of ten to twelve inches across the top. Of course, lengths must vary accord ing to the window, or series of windows, or railing to be decorated.The most common material for window boxes is woodCalifornia redwood, which becomes a neutral gray if notpainted, and cypress will last for years. Cedar is recommended, as is a good grade of white pine. Other materialsinclude metals, which are attractive and, for the most part, light in weight. However, they have the disadvantage of conducting heat, thus overheating the soil. Other suitable and durable lightweight materials are plastic, fiberglass, spun glass, and Gardenglas.

Instead of window boxes, shelves-wide boards with holes to support pots at the rims-can be attached to windows. Here plants are easily changed to keep up a colorful appearance. Consider though that potted plants on shelves dry out quickly.

If you are handy with tools, you can make your own boxes of wood, following instructions in pamphlets from your agricultural experiment station. Whatever plan you follow, get boards one to one and a quarter inches thick. (Thinner boards will warp and offer little insulation against summer heat.) To fasten, rely on brass screws rather than nails, which in a few years may push out and cause a box to fall apart. To make corners secure, reinforce with angle irons. Be sure to provide enough drainage holes in the bottom for water to pass through freely. Space half-inch holes six to eight inches apart.

When boxes are completed, treat the insides with a preservative to prevent rotting. Cuprinol or some other non-toxic material is excellent, but avoid creosote which

ILLUSTRATION XXVII
Impressive array of window boxes at the home of Mrs. A. Deschenes of Montreal Canada

is poisonous to plants. After the preservative has dried, apply at least two coats of good paint or stain.

Painting the Window Box

Select a color which will not detract from the plants. Traditional dark green is satisfactory, though commonplace, unless you use a tint like apple green. Have in mind the colors of the flowers, especially of plants that trail over the sides. Dark flowers do not show up against dark paint, as blue browallia or lobelia against dark green or black. The same is true of white flowers against light surfaces, as white petunias against white or pale yellow boxes.

Since houses are painted various colors, some bright, others dark, window boxes can be colored to match. A light blue house, for example, can have dark blue boxes or boxes in a harmonizing color. Against weathered shingles, blue is pleasing.

On a dark red house with white trim, white boxes with blue and white flowers look well, and in all-white boxes, green and variegated foliage plants are attractive. A white house offers every possibility. Boxes may be of red, pink, lavender, blue, gray, turquoise, or rust, although trim is sometimes a factor.

With a bright color like red, limit flowering plants to one color. I once saw a blue house, with white trimmingsand blue boxes, planted with large hybrid white petunias -a cool, effective combination. Also delightful were blue boxes, with pink geraniums, white alyssum, and blue lobelia on a white house with blue shutters and trim.

Usually with a traditional house conservative green or black boxes look best. These are the colors of the window boxes on Beacon Hill, Boston, chosen to adorn the nineteenth century brick facades. Where the period is not a consideration white or cream-colored boxes look well on brick.

Place Securely

To hold window boxes securely, use bolts or lag screws and treat them beforehand to prevent rusting. Leave an inch or so of space between box and house for the movement of air. If boxes are to rest on a terrace or other solid surface, raise them on cleats or set up on bricks or blocks of wood so drainage holes won't become clogged. Some space under boxes is also important for air circulation, which will dry up run-off water.

When you plant a box, put an inch layer of broken flower pots, crushed brick, small stones or pebbles over the bottom to enable water to escape freely through the openings. Above this, spread a piece of wet burlap or a layer of moist sphagnum moss, old leaves, hard coal clinkers or cinders to prevent soil from washing into the drainage area. If you use cinders, first sift to remove ashes, then break up with hammer or stone into half-inch pieces. These will let water pass through, yet retain moisture and some of the fertilizer that washes down.

Soil and Spacing

Plants in boxes need rich soil for luxuriant growth. Space larger kinds-geraniums, coleus, and fuchsias-eight to ten inches apart; smaller kinds-lobelias, annual phlox, wax begonias, sweet alyssum, and browallia-six inches apart. An eight-inch-wide box accommodates two rows of plants, with the tall ones in back and the low ones along, the front. Boxes, ten inches wide, take three rows of plants, tall, medium, and low for edging.

After planting, spread an inch mulch of peat moss or other mulch over the soil to delay drying out and keep weeds in check. In a month, give a liquid fertilizer and follow up with feedings every seven to ten days. Foliage fertilizers can also be applied, but only as a supplement to root feeding.

Kinds of Plants

The choice of plants for window boxes is limited only by size. Plants over a foot high do not look well unless boxes are exceptionally large. Otherwise, you can grow almost anything you want. For early spring, you might start with Dutch bulbs. In cold regions, these can be purchased already grown, or you can raise your own.

Try hyacinths with pansies or early tulips or daffodils interplanted with grape hyacinths, or basket-of-gold and arabis with scillas, chionodoxas, or leucojum. Include some English daisies and sweet-smelling wall flowers, so common in window boxes in western Europe. Violas, blue phlox, aubretia, and forget-me-nots are other possibilities.

Geraniums Are Tops

The favorite window-box plant is the geranium-red or pink for white, cream, or light or dark blue boxes; white for brown, blue, or red boxes. The familiar trailing variegated vinca is excellent with them. Thriving in sun or shade, the vinca needs constant pinching to prevent it from becoming too long. English and German ivies are other trailers for sun or shade. In the sun, low annuals, dwarf marigolds, lobelias and verbenas make nice edgings as does sweet alyssum, in white, purple or lavender. Petunias vie with geraniums in popularity, and any kind can be planted, though the balcony types have the advantage of trailing gracefully over the sides of boxes.

ILLUSTRATION XXVIII

Multiflora begonias and small-leaved English ivy on a window ledge at the home of Miss Elizabeth Coggin. Both plants grow admirably in shade.

Ageratum brings "blue" to sunny boxes. Annual phlox, cockscomb, lantana, creeping zinnia, rock rose or lam-pranthus, portulaca, dwarf snapdragons, and dwarf dahlias are also lovely for a sunny set-up.

These for Shade

In shade that is open to the sky, as on the north side of a house, coleus grows superbly, with white-and-green kinds a handsome contrast for those with red-and-pink leaves. Coleus luxuriates in a rich, humusy soil and requires plenty of moisture. Pinch to keep bushy, and to improve appearance remove the spiked blue flowers, unless you especially like them. The Trailing Queen coleus is one of the best.

Other shade-tolerant trailing plants include English ivy and its varieties, creeping jenny, Kenilworth ivy, creeping fig, German ivy, variegated gill-over-the-ground, myrtle, wandering Jew, zebrina, achimenes, chlorophytum, star of Bethlehem or Italian bellflower, and strawberry begonia.

Fancy-leaved caladiums do well in shade, but adapt to sun if they are started directly in the sun from bulbs. In cold regions, start tubers indoors in a mixture of sand and peat moss in flats or pots and transfer to window boxes when the weather is warm. Tubers need a temperature of 75 to 80 degrees F. to sprout, and will remain inactive for weeks if kept too cool. Tubers may also be planted directly in boxes when the weather warms up, but will take several weeks to make a display.

Patience plant or patient Lucy-in shades of soft rose, pink, peach, scarlet, red, and white-thrives at northern exposures. For trailers you can consider vinca or wandering Jew, either green or variegated, also the silver and purple-leaved zebrina. Tuberous begonias are outstanding performers in window boxes, the large-flowering kinds, with dwarf multifloras along the front.

Hanging tuberous begonias create lovely cascade effects in part or filtered shade.

Other plants for shady or partially shady boxes include browallia, with purple cup-shaped flowers, torenia, thun-bergia or black-eyed-Susan vine, pansy, and nemesia. The red, pink, and white wax or semperflorens begonias combine well with grape or kangaroo ivies. A pleasing pair consists of wax begonias and wandering Jew, and these can be rooted from cuttings of indoor plants.

All these plants resent reflected sun from stone or brick facades, but remain crisp and healthy in shade or part shade.

Summer Home for House Plants

Window boxes offer a summering-out place for house plants, provided they are kept out of the scorching sun. Pots can be rested directly in boxes and packed with peat moss to anchor them and prevent excessive drying. Or cuttings can be taken early in spring to insure a head start. Good trailers among house plants are heart-leaved philodendron, scindapsus, chlorophytum or spider plant, star of Bethlehem, variegated English ivies, strawberry begonia, zebrina, achimenes, German ivy, and lantana, which, though sun-loving, also thrives in partial shade.

Other house plants suitable for outdoor boxes include nephthytis, ferns (with these alone you can do a great deal), alternantheras, foliage begonias, fuchsias, small dracenas, dumb canes, alocasias, maricas, prayer plant, peperomias, asparagus fern, shrimp plant, crown-of-thorns, and bromeliads. If packed in boxes but left in their pots, they can be brought indoors for winter, or cuttings from them can be rooted for the indoor garden.

If you wish, you can combine hardy foliage plants, like pachysandra with trailing myrtle. You might try hostas, though these are really better in larger boxes or tubs. Ferns, both tender and hardy, green and variegated gout-weed, ajuga, artemisia Silver Mound, and variegated gill-160

ILLUSTRATION XXIX

Coleus in a shady window box. Striking results can be achieved
when coleus of different colors are combined.

over-the-ground await the imagination of the enthusiastic window-box gardener.

Evergreens and Berried Branches for Winter

Winters need not be dull. After annual plants are lifted, evergreen branches can be inserted in the soil. These will last until spring, when it is time to set out the first pansies. Branches of balsam fir, white pine, red, Scotch, or black pines, and Douglas fir stay green all winter. Spruce and hemlock will shed their needles when it gets too warm, but replacements can be made. In warm areas such broad-leaved evergreens as podocarpus, pit-tosporum, leucothoe, mahonia, and bull-bay magnolia last several weeks and can be replaced from the abundant supply in the garden.

Berries can be added to the greens. Bittersweet is one of the best, but red alder also stays plump and fresh outdoors. Always colorful are California pepper berries, nan-dina, sea buckthorn, and love apples. Cones and gilded or silvered seedpods and branches are festive at Christmas, with artificial berries and fruits as other possibilities. Where squirrels are not a problem, window boxes can also be turned into feeding stations for winter birds.

Small Evergreens

Of course, window boxes can be directly planted with small evergreens, needled or broad-leaved. Dwarf Japanese yews are excellent, but small junipers and spruces, bear-berry, leucothoe, leiophyllum, pieris, pachistima, rounded arborvitae and boxwood, where not subject to winter injury, are also candidates. In spring, these evergreens can be planted in the garden and room left again for summer-flowering plants. Or you might have two sets of boxes, one for summer and one to set along the terrace perhaps and bring back for winter.

Large window boxes on firm foundations can be partially planted with small evergreens for year-round green, with geraniums, petunias and other flowering plants added for summer color. In this case, boxes must be large enough to accommodate both groups of plants. Such boxes, often made of concrete, adorn hotels, department stores, restaurants, and business offices as permanent features at windows and doorways.

If you plan to grow evergreens in your window boxes in winter, remember that the plants will need water. In warm sections, where camellias, pittosporum, podocarpus, osmanthus, dwarf hollies, nandina and others are hardy, the soil does not often freeze solidly. Despite cold weather, watering, though less frequent than in summer, is needed. In the rush of the holiday season, this chore is too often overlooked.

When Soil Freezes

In the North, where soil freezes it cannot be regularly watered. Meanwhile plants are constantly evaporating moisture that they are unable to replace. This causes windburning and sunscald. It can be somewhat mitigated by heavy watering whenever there is a slight thaw. These will give roots sufficient moisture for another period of freeze. Gardeners often think that plants in containers do not require watering in winter. This explains why evergreens in window boxes, tubs, and planters are unsightly or dead by spring.

If you do not decorate your boxes in winter, if possible remove and store them until spring. This will prolong their life considerably, for thawing and heaving place a strain on wood or other material. Harmful, too, is the constant exposure to moisture, sun, snow, and ice. Dump soil out, if more is easily obtained in spring, and store boxes in dry place. In winter clean and repair them and apply a fresh coat of paint or stain.

PLANTS FOR WINDOW BOXES IN SHADE OR PARTIAL SHADE

Fancy-leaved caladiums with German or English ivies or
heart-leaved philodendron Ferns and coleus with sprenger
asparagus Multiflora tuberous begonias and small-leaved English
ivy Patience plant and torenia with vinca or English ivy Pink or
red wax begonias and variegated vinca Red and white wax
begonias with green or variegated wandering Jew

Upright coleus and coleus Trailing Queen Upright coleus and
vinca or English ivy Upright and hanging tuberous begonias
Upright and trailing fuchsias Upright fuchsias and star of
Bethlehem, both blue and white White, pink, and red wax
begonias alone or with German or English ivies

PLANTS FOR WINDOW BOXES IN THE SUN

Calendulas with lantanas California poppies with
ageratum Dwarf marigolds with ageratum and
vinca Geraniums with petunias and vinca

Geraniums with ageratum or lobelia and vinca

Geraniums with German or English ivies

Geraniums and lantanas

Geraniums with variegated gill-over-the-ground

Geraniums with lobelia or ageratum and annual phlox

Ivy geraniums and double petunias

Lantanas with ageratum or lobelia

Lantanas with dwarf marigolds

Petunias with verbenas

White geraniums with dwarf salvia and lobelia

Zonal and ivy-leaved   geraniums

15. HANGING BASKETS FOR GRACE

Hanging baskets and pots are charming garden features, whether part of the container garden or simply decoration for an entrance or porch. Suspended at various heights, baskets make it possible to grow plants in midair, where at eye level, or above, they can be enjoyed for their graceful beauty.

Fuchsias, with their pendent, jewel-like blossoms, tuberous begonias, lantanas, and star of Bethlehem take on a new look when seen from below. Even a nondescript trailer, weedy at that, creeping jenny or creeping charlie, looks entirely different in a basket. In fact, if you grow it, you will often be asked what it is.

To decorate porches or balconies, plants in baskets are delightful, but they can also be suspended on fences, walls, poles, beams of garden shelters, and from the eaves of a garage, tool shed or garden house. Lampposts, poles, arbors, and pergolas are other appropriate locations, not to mention the branches of trees.

Plants in baskets require no special care, and are just as simple to care for as plants in pots or boxes. The easiest way is to purchase planted baskets from florists or garden centers, but it is also fun to make your own baskets and plant them.

Kinds of Baskets

A hanging basket may consist of a wire frame lined with moss and filled with soil. Or the effect of a basket may be obtained by suspending a flower pot in a wire holder or by wires drawn through holes made at the pot rim. Glazed and unglazed pottery, wooden baskets or tubs, plastic pots, and slatted wooden frames can also be suspended.

On the West Coast, slatted frames of redwood or cedar are recommended because they hold moisture better than wire frames. These frames may be square, octagonal, round, or triangular. For walls, fences, or other vertical surfaces, there are baskets made with one flat side.

To reduce evaporation, clay pots may be painted or shellacked. Keep to soft colors that do not detract from the plants. Open wire baskets are durable and nonbreak-able, but those made of copper are best because they do not rust. Wire baskets are inexpensive, and if you plant your own, the cost is negligible.

Moss Lining for a Basket

The first step in planting a wire or slatted basket is to line the inside with moss. This holds soil in place and also provides a drainage layer. You can gather moss in the woods, selecting large patches that can be rolled off in big pieces. When you line a basket with this, let the green side face out.

Sphagnum moss, obtainable from a florist, is a good liner, because, even when wet, it holds a lot of air. If you start with dry moss, before placing it, moisten it well with a solution of weak fertilizer for the benefit of the plant roots. Osmunda fiber, procurable at garden centers, is a good substitute for sphagnum, because it decays slowly, but it has the disadvantage of drying out quickly and is an unattractive dark color. Because Osmunda is springy, pack it firmly so drainage will be adequate.

At the base of the wire frame, you can insert a saucer to catch excess water. This will then hold a supply of moisture for roots, and the saucer will prevent a drip-through to porch or terrace.

Some types of baskets, among these clay, come with saucers attached.

How to Plant a Basket

To grow plants only in the center of a moss-lined basket, fill with soil and plant with care. For immediate effects, select fairly large plants, all ready to bloom. You can add hanging plants, ivy or vinca, at the edge, with upright growers-wax begonias or zonal geraniums-in the center for height. This is a simple variation from the typical hanging plant of ivy-leaved geranium, lantana, fuchsia, or tuberous begonia.

With some kinds, strawberry begonia and star of Bethlehem (called also Italian bell-flower), you will want plants to creep down the sides of the basket for a cascade. For this, first place moss in the basket and spread soil to the halfway mark. Through the wire openings at the sides, insert young plants, laying them carefully on the sides. Then pack soil around the root balls. Repeat higher up, adding more moss, soil and plants until you reach the top center where larger specimens will be planted upright. At the surface, make a central depression to catch water.

Fertilizing Basket Plants

After planting, suspend the basket in a barrel of water, a pail or a garden pool up to the rim until it absorbs enough moisture for the surface to feel wet. Then hang up the basket to dry. Or dip it in a weak fertilizer solution if you did not soak the moss previously. After this treatment, feeding will not be needed for two weeks. Thereafter, dip the basket in a fertilizer solution once a week. This method enables plant food to spread throughout the moss lining. If you prefer, you can feed plants with a solution poured over the soil surface.

For baskets, use the soil mixture recommended for window boxes, unless plants require something special.

Tuberous begonias and fuchsias, with their fine fibrous roots, should not be allowed to dry out. Generally, they will need watering twice, perhaps three times, a day in very hot weather. If possible, arrange baskets on pulleys so they can be lowered easily for you to touch the soil and determine how much to water. Or keep a small ladder handy for this purpose.

For plants exposed to constant sun and wind, the pot-in-basket technique is helpful. This consists of placing a potted plant in a basket and surrounding it with peat moss, which can be readily kept moist. You can do the same with clay or other solid-type baskets. Plants will remain moist much longer with this method.

Trailing house plants can be grown in hanging baskets, but most popular are the hanging types of geraniums, fuchsias, and tuberous begonias, which are discussed here in separate chapters.

The Graceful Achimenes

A favorite basket plant in the South is the delicate achimenes. With attractive, oval-shaped leaves and tubular flowers in violet, blue, pink, scarlet, and white, this relative of the gloxinias and African violets thrives through long, hot, humid summers. Some good varieties are the large-flowering Mauve Queen, the pale blue Adelaide and Cattleya, Pink Beauty, Purple King, and the white Jaureguina Maxima and Margaritae, also called Purity.

Achimenes is also well adapted to hanging baskets in the North, where it grows rapidly during the hot days of a shorter summer. Plants need an indoor start to insure early bloom. Start small, scaly, sprouting tubers in large pots or trays in March or April. If no growth is visible, spread the tubers on moist Vermiculite, sawdust, sphagnum moss, or screened peat moss, and keep at 70 to 90 degrees F. until sprouts appear.

For a good starting medium, mix equal thirds of leaf-mold, peat moss, and sharp sand. Scatter tubers over this and cover with one-quarter-inch of the mixture. Tubers thus started in flats or pots can be moved to permanent quarters when plants are one-half to two inches high. Through this early growing period, keep moist but not wet at 70 to 75 degrees if possible.

You can also start achimenes in the baskets in which they will grow. Plant the sprouted tubers in a mixture of two parts leaf mold, one part soil, one part peat, one-half part sharp sand and one quarter part sifted sphagnum. For each bushel of mixture, add a three-inch pot of dry manure and half this amount of bone meal, and be certain you have sufficient drainage material at the bottom of the container. Plant five to six tubers in a six-inch hanging basket and ten to twelve in a twelve-inch basket or twenty to twenty-five in a sixteen-inch basket. A four-inch basket can accommodate three to five bulbs. When planting, keep tips pointed outward and cover with three-quarter-inch of soil.

Achimenes can be taken outdoors when temperatures are likely to remain above 60 degrees F. Growth will be rapid once it starts. When plants are six inches high, top-dress with an inch of peat moss and a small amount of dry manure. Feed bulbs every ten to fourteen days with a weak solution of liquid fertilizer. The usual amount recommended for pot plants, one teaspoon of a complete chemical fertilizer to a gallon of water, is excellent.

At the end of the season, when lower leaves start to wither, plants go into a dormant period. Withhold water gradually, and cut off stems when tops have withered. In cold regions, bring indoors before frost. After foliage is gone, tubers may be left where they are and stored at 50 degrees F. Or they can be taken out of the soil and stored in dry sand or Vermiculite. The same achimenes will grow successfully in the same containers for three seasons. After that they will need separating and replanting in a fresh soil mixture.

   Toward the end of the growing season, small growths or tubers will appear at the axils of the leaves. You can gather these before they fall and grow them to flowering size, first sprouting them on a moist medium. These new tubers will take longer to start because they are covered with a waxy substance.

   Given a humusy soil, warmth and good air circulation, freedom from drafts and shelter from high wind, achimenes will perform magnificently all summer. Since watering with cold water spots the leaves, have it tepid, but avoid wetting the foliage. As shade lovers, achimenes will scorch in hot sun, but the weak sun early or late in the day or filtered sunshine is needed for bloom. During the growing period, keep moist as you do African violets.

SOME EXCELLENT PLANTS FOR HANGING BASKETS

Achimenes Annual phlox Bindweed
   (Convolvulus cneorum) Boston Fern Browallia Ceropegia
Chlorophytum Coleus, Trailing Queen Columnea
   (C. gloriosa & hirta) Creeping Jenny Dianthus Dimorphotheca
Donkey-Tail Sedum Dwarf French Marigolds Episcia
   (E. chontalensis & fulgida) English Ivy Felicia
Fern Asparagus Flowering Maple Fuchsia

German Ivy

Gill-over-the-Ground

Grape Ivy

Ivy-leaved Geranium

Kangaroo Ivy

Kenilworth Ivy

Lantana

Lobelia

Lotus
(Lotus bertheloti) Mahernia Manettia Monkey flower

Nasturtium Nierembergia Oxalis

Petunia-Balcony Types Philodendrons Poor Man's Weather Glass
(Anagallis arvensis caerulea)

Portulaca Pothos or Scindapsus

Rosary Vine

Schizanthus

Shrimp Plant

Sprenger Asparagus

Star of Bethlehem or Italian Bell-Flower *(Campanula isophylla)*

Strawberry Begonia

Sweet Alyssum

Thunbergia or Black-eyed-Susan-Vine Torenia or
Wishbone Flower Vinca Wandering Jew or Inch Plant

Zebrina

16. ROOFTOP GARDENS

Whether on one-story structures or on skyscrapers, rooftop gardens are havens with a charm of their own. For the owners, they provide private worlds in which to grow plants and escape the bustle of city life. All this, of course, is made possible with soil brought in and carried to the top of the building for the pots and boxes that comprise the rooftop garden. If you have ever seen a penthouse garden, you know what a feeling of space it gives, especially if the building is high. It is like being on a mountain top, with a panoramic view that on clear days seems limitless.

Build Windbreaks

Delightful as these skyline gardens are, they do present problems. The wind, for example, snaps trees and tears up plantings. Arrangements must be made to provide shelter in the form of fences or other barriers. These also give needed privacy. Winds constantly dry out the soil so that in summer when the sun is hot, plants often need watering two or three times a day. Pergolas, lattice fences, wood panels, and laths can be erected to provide shade but still allow air and sun to enter.

Winter cold is another problem. In cold regions, where soil freezes solidly, evergreen plants are often wind burned through loss of moisture that is hard to replace when the soil is frozen. The sun, too, draws off moisture and causes sunscald. Rooftop gardens only a few stories up are less affected by wind and are often easier to care for than plantings on the ground. They are usually protected by buildings on one or more sides and get sun for only a part of the day.

Roof Must be Strong

At the start make certain the roof is strong enough to support the weight of containers filled with soil. Modern buildings usually are, but you will be wise to have your structure checked by a building inspector. Then make sure that water can be drained away through pipes. Most important, build a wall around the edge of the roof high enough to serve as a guard. This can be constructed with some harmonizing materials such as concrete, brick, and wood.

The next step is to make a plan. On the whole, simple, formal designs are best in the limited area of a roof. Allow for some large boxes for trees and shrubs and for planters or raised beds, which will give the feeling of flower borders. Erect fences and lay out several enclosed areas for dining, sunbathing, and reading.

Only those who have lugged soil in baskets and boxes onto elevators or up flights of stairs know what this involves, yet without it there can be no garden. If you go to all this effort, obtain good soil, since the labor and cost for good and bad soil are about the same. As for containers, be certain they are large enough to hold sufficient earth. Shrubs, vines, and roses need a depth of eighteen inches; trees need considerably more. For perennials, annuals, and bulbs, a depth of ten to twelve inches is satisfactory. If boxes are equipped with wheels, it will be easy to move them around and water will pass through the holes without interference.

Since rooftop space is limited, try to have boxes fit specific areas. Here is your opportunity to introduce interesting shapes suited to the overall design. If you set up boxes in step fashion, you can grow more plants in a limited area. Allow some space for vines and espaliered plants to cover walls, fences, and other vertical surfaces.

Instead of adding soil to all the containers, fill a few of the largest with moist peat or sphagnum moss. Flowering potted plants can be plunged directly into these and be replaced when they are past their prime. This may be expensive, but it always seems worthwhile, and you do not have to replace a large amount of worn-out soil after a period of years.

Containers for Rooftops

All kinds of containers are suited to the roof garden. Glazed pots stay moist longer than clay, as do wooden tubs and boxes, which keep soil cool. If containers are not heavy enough to stand up in wind, they will need securing. Light plastic pots have to be reinforced by being closely grouped or placed in tubs, jardinieres, or planters.

With so much wall space, think what you can do with wall brackets. Try grouping pots of the same size, including some trailing English ivy or the weeping variety of lantana. Hanging baskets can be attached to walls if these are not exposed to strong wind. When suspending plants on walls, avoid positions from which they might fall on someone. Secure the pots with strong hooks and wire and keep them low enough to make watering easy.

Trees for Height

Every rooftop garden requires a tree or so for height. They also add interest of foliage and blossoms. Willows, which are fast growing and resilient, have been used successfully. When they get too large for their containers, they are easily replaced. Oriental flowering cherries, crab-apples, apple, pear, ailanthus, silk tree, linden, birch and upright maples or lindens for slender height are all good trees for rooftop gardens in the North.

Plan for some evergreen trees and shrubs for year-round color and mass. Scotch, mugo, and Japanese black pines, hollies, Japanese yews, pieris, mountain laurel, camellias, azaleas, and rhododendrons will flourish with some protection. Among the deciduous shrubs, privet, forsythia, spirea, firethorn, mock-oranges, lilacs, and viburnums have proved their worth.

Vines for Patterns

Vines cover bare walls and provide flower and foliage patterns. Wisteria is one of the best; but Japanese honeysuckle, bittersweet, the fast-growing Chinese fleece vine, Boston ivy, and Virginia creeper or woodbine are all excellent. English ivy, as a climber or ground cover, will hold its own on rooftops, though it must be kept out of strong winter sun in the North. Scarlet runner beans, morning glories, cypress vine, and moon flowers are annual kinds to try.

Roses for Fragrance

Every rooftop garden, even the smallest, should have some roses for color and fragrance, as well as their ability to take wind. Train some climbers over the walls and concentrate on such floribundas as Betty Prior, Pinocchio, Carrousel, Floradora, Spartan, Vogue, and Fashion. Miniature roses are ideal for small containers or for edging larger planters. You'll like the pink Sweet Fairy, the deep crimson Tom Thumb, the yellow Bit O'Sunshine, and Pink Joy. Rotiletti, a rose-pink that is one of the hardiest, grows six inches tall.

Some perennials are essential, so make room for day-lilies, astilbes, iris, veronicas, shasta and painted daisies, balloon flowers, hostas and chrysanthemums. If climate allows, plan for spring bulb displays of crocus, hyacinths, daffodils, and tulips. During the summer all kinds of tender bulbs can be grown-dwarf dahlias, tigridias, gladiolus, montbretias, Peruvian daffodils, calla lilies, and fancy-leaved caldiums. Hardy lilies can be bought as pot plants in early spring for setting out in suitable containers.

Annuals will provide riotous color, so allow for some of these-marigolds, zinnias, petunias, nicotiana, nierembergia, Madagascar periwinkle. *(Vinca rosea),* cleome, snapdragons, annual phlox, verbena, dimorphotheca, ageratum, and heat-loving portulaca. Coleus will thrive in shade, and heliotrope will give fragrance. Fuchsias and geraniums offer vivid splashes of color; and in the constant wind and intense sunshine of the rooftop, succulents and sedums are without peer.

The concentrated area of the roof garden offers opportunity to display attractive containers. There you can give prominence to a handsome decorated jar, a choice piece of glazed pottery, or a hand-carved wooden tub. On the wall, you might hang a bird cage filled with foliage plants or a hand-painted pot with grape or kangaroo ivy. Beside a doorway, place a glazed strawberry jar planted with sedums and succulents or an ornamental well-head with trailing grape ivy will be attractive.

A Boston Rooftop Garden

A delightful example of a roof garden is that of Mr. and Mrs. Joel E. Harrell of Commonwealth Avenue, Boston. Located on the seventh floor of their modern apartment, the thirty-one- by twenty-five-foot tiled terrace commands views of the Commonwealth Avenue Mall, the Boston Public Garden and the city's picturesque rooftops and chimneys. Sheltered by the apartment on two sides, there is a four-foot brick wall along the edge of the other sides

ILLUSTRATION XXX

A glimpse of the pleasant rooftop garden of Mr. and Mrs. Joel
E. Harrell in the early winter. In the summer, geraniums and
other annuals are grown among the evergreens.

ILLUSTRATION XXXI
Petunias and nasturtiums in plant boxes on the rooftop of a
section of Mrs. Robert Cushman's home in Beacon Hill, Boston.

to cut the force of the wind and give privacy to the sitting area.

Lined along the wall are natural redwood tubs and planters, with Japanese yews, mountain laurel, pieris, junipers, Hinoki cypress, azaleas, and trailing Baltic ivy. There are eleven planters and six large octagonal tubs. Though this is primarily an architectural, easy-to-main-tain green garden, in the summer, geraniums, ruffled white petunias, and blue lobelias are planted in front of the evergreens. On the axis of the glass living-room doors stands a charming figure of a little girl holding a large bowl above her head. The bowl is kept filled with water for the birds and the figure stands in a small pool with pots of English ivy instead of water. Two lead fan-tailed pigeons complete the composition. Sometimes potted flowering plants, like white chrysanthemums in the fall, brighten the picture.

According to Mrs. Harrell, all the soil was brought up by elevator in wheelbarrows and boxes. After containers were filled, humus was added, and each year a few inches of old soil is removed from the top and replaced with fresh mixture. The evergreens are fed twice a year-a heavy application in the early spring and a lighter one in the fall. Plants are watered daily during the growing season. Shade is provided by a large fireproof awning of dark green.

Because of its good design, this three-year-old rooftop terrace is equally lovely in winter. In fact, the Harrells like it best just after a light snowstorm. At Christmas, the statue is moved to one side to make room for a lighted and tubbed Christmas tree which adds lively color to this rooftop haven.

17. PLANTERS FOR PERMANENCE

A relatively new feature in gardens is the planter. Contemporary houses are frequently designed with built-in planters, and traditional types have them at entranceways, on terraces, and beside garages. On the West Coast especially, many houses and gardens include planters of such durable materials as concrete, brick, or blue stone.

There are two types-the permanent planter attached to the house and the movable one bought or built to suit a particular need. Some gardeners maintain several for replacement as plants pass their prime. Planters are rectangular, square, oblong, triangular, hexagonal, circular, or free form. Like pots and tubs, their value is largely architectural.

Permanent Kinds

Stationary planters outdoors must be planned with care. Those attached to entranceways or the front of a house should be designed in proper scale and proportion, and with good drainage facilities at the start, for unlike the portable type, they cannot be moved or easily replaced. It 188

159

ILLUSTRATION XXXII

Modern-styled triangular boxes, constructed of redwood, in an intimate contemporary patio. (Courtesy: California Redwood Association)

ILLUSTRATION XXXIII
Redwood retaining walls in California-style garden with masses of
Easter lilies and hydrangeas. Large groupings of flowers create the
effect of bed.

is important not to place them over ledges or other obstructions through which water cannot easily pass. Usually these planters are open to the ground. If the soil is clayey, some should be removed and replaced with a layer of stones or cinders to insure drainage.

Movable Kinds

Mobile planters can be carried, pushed, or wheeled to various positions. Desirable construction materials include wood-with redwood, cedar and cypress heading the list-metals, fiberglass, plastic and various synthetic products. Whatever you buy, make yourself or have made, be certain beforehand that you know what the material looks like, how it behaves under your weather conditions and how durable it is. A greater investment in the beginning will pay off in the end.

Choosing the Plants

When selecting the plant material, give thought to scale. In large planters, trees and shrubs, including needle and broad-leaved evergreens, should be grown. With annuals, rely on tall kinds, like cosmos, African marigolds and cleome. If planters are long, repeat one of the plants for unity and harmony. Usually some trailing plants are needed along the edge to soften it.

The permanent planter requires trees and shrubs for year-round effect. Except in the very large planters attached to big buildings, rely on small or dwarf types. Among trees for colder climates, consider Japanese maple and its varieties, ornamental magnolias, flowering cherries, including the weeping forms, Tatarian maple, flowering dogwood, birches, dwarf forms of Scotch, red, and Japanese black pines, upright arborvitaes and junipers and fastigiate trees, as the upright European hornbeam or linden. The flowering crabs are superb, especially the white-flowering Sargent, which remains low and spreading.

Among evergreen and deciduous shrubs, there are the Japanese yews, spreading and ground-cover types of junipers, dwarf arborvitae, shrubby evergreen euonymus, skimmia, cherry laurel, mahonias, leucothoe, dwarf Hin-oki cypress, the convex-leaved and other hollies, camellias, azaleas, slender deutzia, dwarf rhododendrons, fothergilla, flowering quinces, heathers, and the mugo pine. Good barberries include the Wintergreen *(Berberis julianae)*, Korean *(B. koreana)*, Mentor *(B. mentorensis)*, three-spine *(B. triacanthophora)*, and warty *(B. verruculosa)*. The dwarf forms of the Japanese barberry, including Crimson Pygmy and the low *Berberis thunbergi minor,* are superior plants.

ILLUSTRATION XXXIV

Custom-made planters, joined with a picket fence and gate, across the driveway of Mr. and Mrs. Moses Alpers. Planters, provided with wheels, are moved to an unused corner of the garage in winter. Note the pot plants on the driveway beyond.

ILLUSTRATION XXXV

Cotoneasters are valuable because they stay small, have attractive foliage and red berries, develop a loose, informal habit, grow in a variety of situations and withstand wind. Certainly worth considering are the bearberry *(Coton- easter dammeri)*, rock spray (C. *horzontalis)*, the small-leaved cotoneaster *(C. microphylla)*, and the delightful prostrate form, *Cotoneaster adpressa.*

Several specimens of trees or shrubs make a pleasing combination with one type of ground cover or trailer, like dwarf Japanese yew with English ivy, Korean boxwood with myrtle, or dwarf Hinoki cypress with pachysandra. Other good ground covers to combine with evergreens include pachistima, prostrate junipers, bearberry or arcto-staphyllos, yellowroot, sweet fern, trailing euonymus, as the purple-leaf type *(Euonymus fortunei coloratus)*, leio-phyllum or sand myrtle, ajuga, and various thymes and sedums.

Flowers for Color

Planters also need flowers for color. You can start with spring bulbs, like daffodils and tulips, continue with annuals, and finish the season with chrysanthemums. For a pleasing edging, there is the permanent English ivy. Except for small planters, flowering plants are best combined with shrubs. For planters that are three feet or longer, petunias and geraniums, though colorful, are not tall enough.

ILLUSTRATION XXXVI

Geraniums in a blue-stone planter in the terrace wall of Mrs. Ann Esancy. A hole at the side at the base serves as a drainage outlet.

ILLUSTRATION XXXVII

A corner of a California garden, with redwood retaining wall and boxes with trees, shrubs and flowering plants. (Courtesy: California Redwood Association)

Built-in types look well with tropical foliage and flowering plants, which are summer subjects in the North. In sun, for example, the bold leaves of rubber plants (include a few of the variegateds), small palms, Japanese aralia, large-leaved philodendrons, scheffleras, alligator pears and pandanus look well together. Smaller kinds- crotons in variety, hibiscus, grevillea, brunfelsia, and flowering maples-offer spots of color.

Cannas, with huge, bold leaves, have a modern look. Hybrid angel's trumpets, with large leaves and dramatic white flowers, are dynamic. In smaller planters, dwarf varieties of cannas-Pfitzer's Cherry-Red, Pfitzer's Primrose Yellow, and Pfitzer's Shell Pink-are more desirable. Castor bean, difficult to place because of its enormous leaves, is excellent for the large planters of contemporary houses, as is elephant's ear, started easily from tubers.

These for Shade

In partial shade or filtered sunlight, the variety can be even greater. Start with the clean-cut modernistic lines of large-leaved philodendrons-*Philodendron dubia*, *P. has-tatum*, or *P. jaciniatum*. Many other philodendrons are suitable. Tall and medium kinds give height, and thetrailing, heart-leaved philodendron, will fall gracefully over the edge of a planter.

The long list of suitable tropicals includes dracaenas, dieffenbachias, Chinese rubber plants, foliage begonias like the rex types, aglaonemas, anthuriums, aphelandra, ardisia, aucuba, bromeliads, cissus, crotons, ficus, ferns, peperomias, pothos, nephthytis, spathiphyllum, syngo-nium, and tradescantias. Consider also the fancy leaves of alocasias, many with bizarre patterns. In planters, you can group the tropical foliage plants you grow indoors in winter by inserting the pots in damp peat moss or Vermiculite.

For Warm Regions

In warm areas, with little or no freezing, tropical plants can be grown outdoors all year round. Delightful in Florida are crotons, and there are so many varieties, with odd leaf forms and colors, some that even look like different plants. Easy to grow, they withstand neglect and pruning. Camellias, tender hollies, Chinese hibiscus, gardenias, poinsettias, pittosporum, clivias, agapanthus, bamboos, podocarpus, loquat, citrus, tender azaleas, sansevieria, cymbidium and other orchids, fancy-leaved caladiums, bird of paradise, epiphyllums-all have exciting possibilities for planters in the South.

18. CONTAINER PLANTS IN PLACES OF BUSINESS

Flower-filled window boxes, tubs and planters are today an attractive feature of more and more places of business, both small and large. Shopping centers, department stores, dress shops, banks, insurance companies, hospitals, art and specialty shops, grocery stores, filling stations, even factories are now decorated with container plants. Restaurants, particularly at resorts, hotels, motels, and tourist homes also employ this method of attracting business.

Europe Takes Lead

In this aspect of container gardening, Europe has taken the lead. Bank buildings of London, Dublin, Edinburgh, and Paris feature window boxes of azaleas in spring, geraniums in summer, and chrysanthemums in fall. Pink and blue hydrangeas, favorite flowers in Paris, bedeck the facade of the showroom of the Renault automobile on the Champs Elysees, as well as the fashionable restaurants and department stores that line the broad boulevards.In London, Austin Reed's Department Store favors apple-green window boxes with multicolored azaleas, and the Bank of Nova Scotia at Waterloo Place features deep rose hydrangeas. Other English cities follow the pattern-in Bath, for instance, where Colmer's Department Store has set up boxes of red zonal and pink ivy geraniums at the edge of the marquee. In Switzerland, hardly a dress 01 watch shop is overlooked and there, I remember the Lu-zerner Kantanalbank in the town of Horw, where red geraniums crept through the iron bars in front of the windows just as they do from balconies all over Spain.

How Boston Does It

Boston recently took up the practice. Three years ago, the marquee in front of Symphony Hall was lined with boxes of geraniums and English ivy to announce the opening of the Pops Concerts, which to Bostonians heralds the arrival of spring. On Beacon Hill, the Bellevue Hotel has planted boxes of Japanese yews and geraniums along the low balustrade at the front. For fifteen years, Filene's Department Store, one of the largest in the city, has maintained boxes along the marquee that covers an entire block. In spite of adverse growing conditions, winter winds and hot summer sun, hemlocks, Japanese yews, pieris, rhododendrons, and English ivy do remarkably

ILLUSTRATION XXXVIII

Raised boxes and urns with geraniums and white petunias across
the long veranda of the Daniel Webster Inn at Franklin, New
Hampshire.

ILLUSTRATION XXXIX
Hanging baskets of cascading lavender lantanas and tubs of blue
hydrangeas in front of Ketchopulos Market in Rockport, Massachusetts.

well. Replacements are made when needed and sometimes artificial flowers are introduced for color. In the past, real flowers were planted among the evergreens-and still are on occasion-but they must take a terrible beating. To water the boxes, a special system has been installed, with a separate valve for each unit.

Fashionable Newbury Street has been beautified with boxes and planters in front of the small smart shops. Sharaf's Restaurant has a raised bed of red geraniums and white petunias around the sign post in the sidewalk. In summer, the large plate glass window is removed and the inside transformed into a tropical garden with flourishing hibiscus, tree fuchsias, philodendrons, coleus, geraniums, ageratum, morning glories, marigolds, wax begonias, periwinkle, and lobelias. Under this arrangement, plants are protected from strong wind and heavy rain.

In Towns

Business places in towns also realize the value of container plants. In Woodstock, Vermont, window boxes of pink geraniums enliven the facade of the Elm Tree Press. The Grille Restaurant has two large north-exposure boxes, with luxuriant geraniums, dwarf marigolds, and vinca. In Beverly, Massachusetts, the Commodore Restaurant is enhanced with eleven artistic boxes, each with

ILLUSTRATION XL
Cheerful beds of petunias on the sidewalk of Travel. Inc. in
Woodstock Vermont

a different combination of plants. Dark blue boxes and shutters offer contrast to the white structure.

Familiar to visitors to picturesque Rockport, Massachusetts, in the summer are the trailing purple lantanas along the front of Ketchopulos Market. Thirty-three years ago, Mrs. Mary Ketchopulos hung a single specimen in one of the arches of the facade which faces northwest. She received so many compliments that the next summer, she added nine more with blue tubs of blue hydrangeas at the base of each post. Here, everything is regularly watered twice a day and three times in very hot weather. Once a week, plants are fed a liquid fertilizer. Over the years, visitors from many states have stopped to admire these container plants.

You can find pot plants adorning the most unexpected places, like lobster shacks and railroad crossings. When I stepped inside the tall fence of the Salem Lumber Company in Salem, Massachusetts, to buy some flag stones, I was delighted to see two long window boxes of geraniums, petunias, ageratum, and vinca in front of the office. The boxes were built and planted by Roy Chase, an employee who wanted "to dress up the office and make it stand out." Every year Mr. Chase, whose hobby is gardening, starts with fresh soil, containing some dry cow manure. He waters the plants every day and feeds them once a month.

ILLUSTRATION XLI
Window boxes with geraniums, petunias, ageratum and vinca at the office of the Salem Lumber Co. in Salem, Massachusetts.

ILLUSTRATION XLII
Wooden boxes, with geraniums and coleus, built around the posts of the roadside stand of the West view Farm in Walpole, New Hampshire.

At Filling Stations

At a Boston filling station, there is a large planter of cut-leaved philodendrons, geraniums, rubber plants, begonias, and English ivy. The gardener is the manager, Alfred Balboni, who began with two small cut-leaved philodendrons given him by his wife, when he started business in 1954. As the plants outgrew their quarters, he had a galvanized metal planter built for them. Wheels were added, so it could be taken to the wash basin for sprinkling, and wheeled outdoors in summer. There are also several luxuriant window boxes along the office window, with coleus, salvias, zinnias, phlox, rex begonias, vincas, petunias, dwarf marigolds, and ageratum. Mr. Balboni says, "The boys like the flowers, too. They don't mind wheeling the planter in and out in spring till the plants get adjusted, or to shade in summer when the sun is hot, or sprinkling the foliage when I don't have time."

Another filling station in Seabrook, New Hampshire, operated by Mr. Clayton H. Kennedy, has petunias at the front and along the borders of the drive-in area in five boxes eight feet long, eight inches high, and ten inches wide. In the bottom of each is a six-inch layer of well-rotted manure and on top of that two inches of soil. Each box gets a pail of water a day, and no additional feeding.Cutting off faded blossoms is a regular chore worked on in intervals of business.

For Shopping Centers

The Northshore Shopping Center in Peabody, Massa chusetts, is an outstanding example of well-stocked plant ers and raised beds, with permanent trees and shrubs and flowering plants inserted for seasonal color. Twenty-five planters are made of brick and open to the ground. They vary from five-foot circular units, each with one flowering tree, to oblongs eighty feet long filled with a great variety of hardy, durable plants-evergreens, shrubs and small flowering trees-all cared for by Mr. John Watkevitch, the gardener. One long planter at the bus stop features columnar maples, junipers, cotoneasters, and colorful annuals. Everywhere there are benches for shoppers to sit and rest.

The Lloyd Shopping Center at Portland, Oregon, comprises seventy blocks of stores with broad malls landscaped with trees, shrubs, annuals, and bulbs. There are pools, pieces of sculpture, benches and hundreds of planters, free standing and built-in, some disguising the lighting and ventilating facilities of the underground parking area. One long row of planters with Pfitzer junipers is suspended over openings that give light to the area below. Another planter is actually an air vent highlighted by a large shore pine, a vine maple, and several floribunda roses.

To make its mall more attractive, the Eastland Shopping Center in Detroit, Michigan, also constructed raised beds and planters. Honey-locusts, hybrid rhododendrons, mollis azalea hybrids, Japanese holly, and pachysandra comprise the plant material with gray-leaved santolina and *Achyranthes brilliantissima* for decorative patterns. Shoppers at the Center linger to enjoy the flowers and rest on the benches.

Care and Security

Container plants at business places require the same care as those in gardens and parks. Personal interest is essential. Too often owners become neglectful once nurserymen or florists have finished their work. Plants must be watered regularly, especially over week-ends, and foliage must be sprayed with the hose to remove dust and soot. Faded flowers should be removed to prolong blooming.

Where containers can be easily shifted, it may be necessary to secure them to their positions. Window boxes, above the heads of passers-by, are not so threatened by vandals as tubs or other small containers at doorways or on sidewalks, where they can be stolen or smashed. To guard against this, fasten them firmly with a strong chain or with hooks and heavy wire. Private houses and apart ments in some sections may also need to do this

19. CITY BEAUTIFICATION WITH BOXES AND PLANTERS

Plant containers make cities and towns more attractive. Often installed and maintained by local governments, but women's clubs and chambers of commerce also cooperate in this civic project. Window boxes on city buildings, plant boxes in front of libraries and courthouses, planters in parks and public gardens, as well as hanging baskets on lampposts, help make a city beautiful.

New buildings are often equipped with planters. Spacious, free-standing types with permanent trees and shrubs now adorn many parks and small squares. In public places, their broad copings provide a resting place for strollers.

Flower Baskets

Flower baskets are charming on the lampposts of the lovely seacoast town of Camden, Maine, probably the first in the country to adopt them. Hanging baskets are now established features of other cities and towns.

ILLUSTRATION XLIII

A few of the twenty-seven rectangular and twenty-five circular planters along the Tremont Street Mall in Boston. Tired shop pers and visitors like to rest on the wide copings.

The Camden project started when Edward Bok admired the flower baskets on the lampposts of Leamington, England. From photographs which he had brought back, he had a local blacksmith make thirteen similar baskets and presented them to the town in 1925. They were planted and cared for by the Camden Garden Club, and during the thirties their number was increased to thirty-three. Secured to the posts with clamps, the baskets are attached high enough not to interfere with tall trucks that park along the curbs.

The baskets are lined with sphagnum moss before planting and then filled with good soil. A local nursery plants and puts them up before Memorial Day and removes the plants in the fall. In the summer, the baskets are watered and fed by firemen, who are paid by the Garden Club. For years, the baskets were filled with greens and red berries for the winter months, but since 1955 they have been enlivened with lighted Christmas trees, a gay sight for motorists who drive through.

This project is the result of the combined efforts of the Camden Garden Club, the town, and the Chamber of Commerce. Though Leamington, England, provided the inspiration, this city no longer has flower baskets. Bombed during the last war, the new concrete lampposts are without such ornament.

ILLUSTRATION XLIV

White chrysanthemums in an urn and in a wall planter in the garden of the First Church in Salem, Massachusetts. Container plants are most attractive in church gardens.

Victoria's Graceful Baskets

Also famous for its hanging baskets is the city of Victoria, the capital of British Columbia, Canada. The lamppost baskets of Camden do not hang, but in Victoria they do; they are suspended twenty inches from the lamp standards on iron arms placed eleven feet or more above the sidewalks and usually parallel to the curb for reasons of safety. Each basket, weighing up to seventy pounds, is thirteen inches wide and eleven inches deep and is constructed of twelve-gauge galvanized wire on a nine-gauge frame.

Since 1937, baskets have decorated Victoria's business districts and sections bordering the picturesque inner harbor. After a trial of various plants these are now grown: the ivy-leaved geranium Enchantress, dwarf petunia Rose Queen, lobelia Sapphire, schizanthus Giant Blotched, dwarf coreopsis Dazzler, viscaria Rose Beauty, Mexican marigold Golden Gem, variegated ground ivy, and nasturtium Hermine Grashoff. Except for geraniums and nasturtiums, all plants are raised from seed. The schizanthus, nasturtiums and petunias are at their height early in the season, the viscaria in July, while the others come later. The soil mixture consists of two parts peat, two parts sand and nine parts sterilized rotted turf loam, supplemented with two ounces of ground limestone, two ounces of superphosphate, and one ounce of sulphate of potash per bushel of mixture.

LLUSTRATION XLV
Plant containers along Fifth Avenue in New York City

Method of Watering

According to Mr. W. H. Warren, Park Administrator, "the baskets are maintained by one man with a right-hand tank truck powered by a take-off gear from the truck's motor. He waters the baskets during the hours of 11 P.M. to 7:30 A.M., six days a week, as he drives along the curb with an aluminum pipe wand shaped like a shepherd's crook. Liquid fertilizer is supplied every two or three weeks in the form of a three pound ammophos (16-20-0) per gallon tank."

To make watering more effective, a two-inch strip of galvanized iron runs around the top of each basket inside the moss and above the soil level. This prevents loss of water over the sides. To conserve moisture, a size thirty-four tin wash basin, treated with roofing cement on the inside and always kept full of water, is attached to the bottom. Baskets are prepared in the greenhouse in April and displayed on the lampposts from early June to early October. The cost for each including the basket,

pan, plants and labor, is $10.00, plus $6.00 each for maintenance.
Five other British Columbia cities have followed Victoria's

ILLUSTRATION XLVI

lead, Nanimo, Vancouver, New Westminster, Kelowna and Vernon. Olympia, Washington, has also set up baskets and recently, Everett, in the same state had a favorable showing for the first time.

Window-Box Competition in Montreal

In the United States and Canada, many organizations sponsor window-box contests to stimulate interest in this simple and effective method of making cities more attractive. The Window Box Competition of Montreal, Canada, is conducted by Mr. Henry Teuscher, Curator of the Montreal Botanical Garden. Every spring, from March to April, the Botanical Garden offers three lectures on window-box gardening in which students prepare and plant at least one box.

According to Mr. Teuscher: "The Window Box Competition has been active for about fifteen years and is still going strong. In the beginning, we had up to one thousand entries, but most so inferior they could not be considered for prizes. Only one hundred prizes were given, and the prize winning boxes were so superior they established high standards. In consequence, only those registered who really had good boxes and so had a chance to get a prize. During the last few years we have rarely had more than 250 entries, but these really were the best in the city."Four silver trophies comprise the donated awards given each year to the owners of the best boxes, and if an entrant receives a trophy for three successive years, he is entitled to keep it. This has happened several times. A bouquet of roses or other flowers is also presented to each of the first four winners, while ninety-six others are given pots of house plants. Mr. Teuscher has a sum of $300.00 to spend on this project, and this covers the expenses of judges and secretarial help.

Civic Beautification in Philadelphia

The Neighborhood Garden Association of Philadelphia was started in 1953 by Mrs. James Bush-Brown, retired Director of the School of Horticulture for Women at Ambler, Pennsylvania, with the purpose of beautifying through window boxes and gardens, the blighted areas of the city. The first year seven garden blocks with four hundred boxes participated. By 1959, the project included 272 blocks and numerous gardens in vacant lots and around individual homes.

When a group decides to improve the appearance of a block, it forms a block unit, enlisting the services of the occupants of the houses. The members make their own boxes, set them up, and fill them with soil. Then the block is assigned to a suburban garden club, whose mem-220

ILLUSTRATION XLVII

Clipped sweet bay trees in attractive wooden boxes. English ivy
serves as a ground cover and softens the edges of the boxes.

bers supply the block with plants and instruct the owners on planting and care. Blocks hold weekly meetings in members' homes, and there is a monthly get-together in a community center.

The Philadelphia project is valuable because it helps to clean up untidy city blocks and makes them attractive with plants. It also teaches community cooperation among the occupants of tenements and apartments. Because of its success, other cities have sent delegates to study the methods. The Tonawanda Project near Buffalo, New York, and the beautification contests of the Beacon Hill Garden Club and the Beacon Hill Civic Association, as well as the Federation of South End Settlements, of Boston have been inspired by the Philadelphia project.

In Boston

Visitors to Boston in recent years have noted the row of planters along the Tremont Street Mall on the Boston Common in the heart of the downtown shopping area. In all there are twenty-seven rectangular brick planters, each eighteen and one half feet long, six feet wide, and twenty inches high with a single outlet for watering. Between them are twenty-five circular brick planters, six feet in diameter and twenty inches high. Each circular bed holds a white flowering crab-apple with a ground cover of evergreen creeping euonymus. The rectangular planters are edged with low Japanese yew, sheared to twelve inches, and some of the beds have patterns of clipped boxwood in the manner of a knot garden. In spring, the beds are gay with 10,000 bulbs of early-flowering tulips, Vermilion Brilliant, Pelican, Rising Sun, and General de Wet. These are replaced with summer-flowering plants-geraniums, begonias, petunias, ageratums, and marigolds. Mr. John Kane, the Superintendent of the Greenhouses of the Boston Park Department, maintains the beds with two full-time gardeners.

The Window Box Contest sponsored jointly by Boston's Beacon Hill Garden Club and the Beacon Hill Association was started in 1958 under the chairmanship of Mrs. Houlder Hudgins. Today, there are more than 350 window boxes on the historic Hill. To aid participants in the project, literature is distributed with instructions on how to make window boxes, how to secure them firmly, how to fill them with soil, what kinds of plants to grow and what care to give. Most important were the plant lists, suggesting the best kinds for sun and shade. Since the Hill is located in the heart of the city, soil was distributed free to all residents who needed it. During the first year, a crew of forty boys delivered the soil in pails, in many instances hauling it up several flights ofstairs to occupants who had no other way of getting it.

Judging each year takes place in late July, when the boxes look their best. At the end of the season, there is a general meeting at which color slides of the boxes are shown and awards are made. There are two grand prizes, one for the "best individual window box on Beacon Hill" and the other for the "best group of two or more window boxes on a single building." The four top prizes consist of two silver trays and two Paul Revere bowls. In addition, potted plants are offered by merchants on the Hill, as well as other donors. There are two prizes in the children's division.

Window boxes, other containers, and pots and tubs at doorways, have made this old section of Boston more distinctive. "A new idea for Boston," read the application blanks, "a contest which combines the fun of gardening with the pleasure of making Beacon Hill a more beautiful and enjoyable place in which to live."

In New York City

Extensive planting of streets and buildings in New York City began in 1956 when Mrs. Mary Lasker persuaded the Park Department to allow her to plant four blocks along Park Avenue with tulips. Amazed at her success, despite the soot and grime, they gave her permission 224

CITY BEAUTIFICATION WITH BOXES AND PLANTERS

to plant twenty-two Park Avenue blocks the next year and there adopted the enthusiastic beautification program known as "Salute the Seasons." Its purpose is to bring beauty to the downtown areas of New York by planting trees, shrubs and flowers and by setting up window boxes and tubs at shops, banks, hotels, museums, and churches. As the theme suggests, flowers are changed according to the season, with pansies and bulbs in spring, geraniums, begonias and other annuals in summer, and chrysanthemums in fall. Offering valuable information, with instructions on kinds to grow and when and where to plant, is a practical booklet prepared under the direction of the New York City Department of Parks in cooperation with the Department of Commerce and Public Events.

In Pittsburgh

A container garden on a grand scale is at Mellon Square Park in Pittsburgh, Pennsylvania. Viewed from above, this almost one and a half acre park presents a magnificent spectacle with its attractive design, well planted beds, and patterned pavements. Mellon Square Park, built in 1955, covers a six-floor underground parking garage for 1000 cars. An eighteen-inch roof holds up containers made of reinforced concrete, capped and facedwith polished Minnesota gray granite. Drainage lines and irrigation pipes for the planters were installed during construction.

The minimum depth of the planters is fourteen inches; here English ivy and trailing euonymus are grown. Other planters, ranging in depth from twenty-four inches to four feet, hold large deciduous trees. Watering is by means of installed bubblers and sprinkler heads, supplemented by considerable hand watering with short sections of hose. Plants are fed a dry complete fertilizer in early spring, followed by applications of liquid fertilizer in late spring and midsummer.

Planting material was selected on the basis of appropriateness for the design and its ability to withstand soot and grime, fumes from automobiles, and wind that sweeps between tall buildings. There are three enormous neatly-sheared Japanese yews, and the trees include European beech, honey-locust, sourwood, little-leaf linden, sweet-gum, sophora, sweet bay magnolia, and crab-apples.

Aronia, azalea Gable Hybrid Orange, Japanese holly varieties, Laland firethorn, hybrid catawba rhododendrons, Hick's Japanese yews, Maries double-file viburnum, English boxwood, and wintergreen barberry are the shrubs in the park. Pachysandra, purple-leaf euonymus, and English ivy varieties, Hahn's Maple Queen and Hahn's Shamrock, are used as ground covers. In spring there is color from bulbs; these are followed by annuals and chrysanthemums for summer and autumn displays. Some tropical plants, crotons, pandanus, acalyphas, shrimp plant, and hibiscus, are in a special box, which is also used for a Christmas tree display. For protection against winter injury, plants are sprayed with Wilt-Pruf in early November when the weather is bright, warm, and sunny.

Beautifully maintained, Mellon Square Park is considered "one of the most outstanding examples of redevelopment in an urban area. Surrounded on all four sides by skyscrapers, the park is a cool and inviting oasis to the tired shopper, the harried executive, and the multitude of workers who are employed in the downtown area."

In the midst of concrete and steel, where gardening in the open ground is not possible, Mellon Square Park represents a large-scale garden created in boxes and planters-an outstanding and successful example of this new gardening concept.

Printed in Dunstable, United Kingdom